You Can Make a Difference

Jack Graham

YOU CAN

MAKE A
DIFFERENCE

BROADMAN PRESS
NASHVILLE, TENNESSEE

© Copyright 1992 • Broadman Press
All rights reserved
4230-10
ISBN: 0-8054-3010-5
Dewey Decimal Classification: 222.8
Subject Heading: BIBLE. O.T. NEHEMIAH
Library of Congress Catalog Card Number: 92-12732
Printed in the United States of America

Library of Congress Cataloging-in-Publication Data

Graham, Jack, 1950-
    You can make a difference / Jack Graham.
        p. cm.
    ISBN 0-8054-3010-5
    1. Bible. O.T. Nehemiah—Sermons.   2. Christian leadership—
Sermons.   3. Southern Baptist Convention—Sermons.   4. Baptists—
Sermons.   5. Sermons, American.   I. Title.
    BS1365.6.L4G73   1992   92-12732
    252′.06132—dc20   CIP

Dedication

To Deb, my wife, and our children Jason, Kelly,
and Josh, whose faithful love truly
makes a difference in my life

Preface

This book is a series of expositions from the Book of Nehemiah delivered at the Prestonwood Baptist Church in Dallas, Texas. Because leadership is the most vital factor in the church, the home, the government, and society at large, these messages from Nehemiah are offered to challenge God's people everywhere to assume purposeful responsibility to make a difference in the realms of their personal influence.

I have been powerfully impacted by the life and journal of this veteran Old Testament leader. The principles expressed in his Spirit-inspired memoirs are as current as the most recent publications on the subject of leadership development.

Authentic, dynamic leaders are needed now more than ever. Whatever your calling in life, I believe the biblical message found within these pages will both encourage and charge you to become the kind of person God can use to rebuild the broken walls which have crumbled all around us. The world is waiting for men and women just like you, who will say, "Let us arise and build!"

This book is offered with the prayer that you will hear that urgent call and make a difference in your world for the sake of the gospel of Jesus Christ.

—Jack Graham

Contents

Contents

You Can Make a Difference

1

You Can Make A Difference

Nehemiah 1:1-4

The forefathers of Saddam Hussein, the Babylonians, had sacked the holy city, Jerusalem, and destroyed it, carrying the children of Israel into seventy years of captivity. The walls were shattered, and the gates were burned.

After years and years of captivity, God, in His providence, allowed a segment, a "remnant," surviving the captivity to travel back to Jerusalem and rebuild the temple of God. Worship was reinstituted in the Holy City, but the city itself was still in ruins. Those demolished walls and burned-out gates lay in silent, constant testimony to Israel's defeat and shame.

Beginning in the very first verse, we discover how one man could make a difference in a seemingly impossible situation.

1 The words of Nehemiah, the son of Hachaliah.
It came to pass in the month of Chislev, in the twentieth year, as I was in Shushan the citadel [that is, Persia], *2* that Hanani one of my breth-

ren came with men from Judah; and I asked
them concerning the Jews who had escaped,
who had survived the captivity, and concerning
Jerusalem. 3 And they said to me, "The survi-
vors who are left from the captivity in the prov-
ince are there in great distress and reproach. The
wall of Jerusalem is also broken down, and its
gates are burned with fire." 4 So it was, when I
heard these words, that I sat down and wept, and
mourned for many days; I was fasting and praying before the God of heaven (Neh. 1:1-4).

Those walls, crumbled and scattered, spoke of
the broken witness of God's people. The walls
around ancient cities were, of course, built for protection. Those walls around the city of Jerusalem,
according to the psalmist, were there as "unto the
praise of God, the city of the great king." Now that
those walls were down, the people were defenseless
and vulnerable. To make matters worse, no one
seemed to care. The fact is, rebuilding can be more
difficult than building from the beginning. Unfortunately, if your marriage is broken, it is easier to
walk away and call it quits than to rebuild that relationship. It is less difficult to give up when your
business has failed than to try and rebuild it. Yes,
that also relates to a church. When a church is broken, when a church is scandalized or shamed,
maybe it is simpler to splinter and split than to rebuild what God has already done.

Four years ago, in 1988, the walls came down
on the Prestonwood Baptist Church. Reproach, distress, and shame dominated. I'm sure that many
felt, "Let's just give up; let's quit." But, thank God,
there was a group of men and women who said,

"We will rebuild the broken-down walls." There were people who cared, who said, "We will do again the work that God has given us." It is the work of rebuilding. By the grace and power of God, the walls have been built.

Nehemiah, what a man! When my mind fixes on Nehemiah, I think of vision, commitment, courage, conviction, compassion, and consistency—all of those. I consider a stalwart man who really cared. It is exciting to be around great men like Nehemiah. Several years ago, when General Westmoreland was the chief of military operations in Vietnam, he was reviewing a group of paratroopers, asking them about their role in Vietnam.

He asked one trooper, "How do you like jumping out of these planes, Son?"

He said, "I love it, can't wait!"

He asked another soldier, "And how do you like jumping?"

He said, "It's the greatest experience of my life, Sir!"

And then he came to the next man and asked the same question, "And what do you think about jumping?"

The young man replied, "I hate it!"

Puzzled, Westmoreland implored, "Well, then, why do you do it?"

"Because I like to be around people that jump!"

When we study Nehemiah, his spirit rubs off on us, because he was a man willing to jump. In the words of William Carey, we are "to attempt great things for God and expect great things from God." Nehemiah did exactly that. Nehemiah made a definite difference. You also can make a difference in rebuilding broken-down walls in your own life and the lives of others.

There are three principles I will share with you regarding *rebuilding the walls* and *making a difference.*

First of all, we must:

Expose the Problem

People who make a difference first face up to the problem. They are not willing to leave well enough alone. They do not have a laissez-faire approach.

Nehemiah asked the question, "How is it in Jerusalem? How are the people there? What is the condition of the great city?" That was significant because we realize Nehemiah lived almost 1,000 miles from Jerusalem in Persia (now Iran). He was a displaced Jew of the captivity—that is, he had himself been taken out of Judah and into captivity. But in his captivity, he had risen to a place of prominence, for we are told in the last verse of this chapter (v. 11) that he was a cupbearer to the king.

That may not sound important to us, but actually, to be cupbearer to the king was one of the most prominent and authoritative positions in all of the ancient world. As the cupbearer to the king, he was in charge of the food and drink served to the king. He was, in other words, the "right-hand man" to the king of Persia. It was his responsibility to make sure that the food and wine were absolutely right. He had to sample the king's food and drink to make sure it was not spoiled or poisoned. He lived in the lap of luxury, enjoying the "good life." He slept, no doubt, in the palace of the king, lying on satin sheets and stuffed pillows. He was a cupbearer to the king, not a priest, not a prophet, but simply a man who cared enough to ask, "How is it in Jerusalem?" When he asked, he received a sobering answer.

So often, our problem is that we want to stay in our comfort zone. We are unwilling to ask what are the needs. The number-one enemy of success is complacency. Some sage put it, "The problem in America is apathy—but who cares?" Many Christians are unaware of what's really happening in the world and in the church. Some refuse to face the facts and expose the problem until we know the facts. The fact *is* the walls are down! In my estimation, these broken-down walls picture the church of Jesus Christ in our era. There is distress and reproach. Christians are under incredible pressure, and therefore many are cracking up. Instead of joy and victory, there is misery and defeat. Lives are broken. Families are fractured. We wonder, *Does anybody care?*

The idea of reproach in the text is one of shame, because ungodly people were mocking. Unbelievers who walked by saw those broken-down walls and burned gates, and they mocked the people of God: "Who is your God? Where is your God? What kind of God do you serve?" Today, people are asking the same question. Our faith is under attack. The walls are down. The enemy rushes in to devour. The jackals of hell are laughing and mocking. It is interesting to me that while the walls were down and the people were in distress, the temple was functioning daily! There were worship, sacrifice, ritual, and routine; and all the while, amid all of that religious exercise, people were going about business as usual. The walls were down, and the Jews did not seem to care. In fact, they were spiritually paralyzed.

People today are asking Christians, "Does your faith really matter?" They see us en route to church; they see our buildings, and they ask, "Can Jesus Christ really make a difference in my life? What happens when my husband walks out? What happens when my kids rebel? What happens when I bury my loved one? What happens when I can't pay my bills? Can Jesus Christ, can your God really make a difference? Do Christians honestly have an answer?" They view our own shame and disgrace. They are aware that our walls are down, that we have not protected ourselves, and that we have not separated ourselves. They chortle at our God because they don't know or believe that He can make a difference. They read the news of our scandals. They view our own walls and wonder if Jesus can make any difference. Many Christians think that our standards of separation and righteousness, those walls, are old and antiquated. The walls are down, and people ask, "What happened?"

The bad news that the walls were down was like a blow to Nehemiah's solar plexus. What bothered Nehemiah the most was that the name of God was being disgraced. Does that matter at all to you? The holiness and the greatness of God were being ridiculed. Nehemiah had a grave concern for the glory of God, and he had to do something about those broken-down walls. He must have wondered, *What can one man do? What can I do, a thousand miles away?* He didn't know yet what he could do, but he knew that he cared, and he cared enough to cry. In verse four, he moaned, "So it was, when I heard these words, that I sat down and wept, and mourned for many days; I was fasting and praying before the God of heaven." Once he exposed the problem, *those broken walls broke his heart.* In the mourning, weeping, and crying, his burden was born. The glory of God and the safety and the security of the people were at stake. The Bible says he mourned for "many days," perhaps months. There is an indication he may have lamented as much as four months—crying, weeping, praying, and fasting. He was so broken and so hurt he couldn't eat. So, he fasted before the Lord. There was no shortcut, and there is no shortcut today. The Bible reminds us that the faithful and fervent prayer of a righteous man avails much (see Jas. 5:16b). God does business with those who mean business with Him!

Yet, Nehemiah's heartbroken concern was quite different from what we recognize in much contemporary Christianity. The health, wealth, and happiness cult contends that the chief purpose of life is to enjoy ourselves, but the Bible teaches us that the reason for living is to give ourselves in service to Jesus Christ. We are not to enjoy ourselves but to employ ourselves in serving our glorious God. For our salvation He died in blood and agony on the cross to give Himself for us—but not for us simply to enjoy the Christian life. Oh, there is ecstatic joy in knowing Jesus, and I want to be happy as much as anyone else, but the purpose in life is not for God to make us happy. The purpose in life is to please Him and make Him happy, and then to *enjoy Him* forever. No sweeping work for God ever begins without brokenness and remorse. We must come to the place in America, in the world, and in the church where we virtually scream, "We can't go on like this anymore! We can't keep doing it the same old way!" I'm afraid that many of us have become so sophisticated, so expert at what we do, so good at business as usual, that if God didn't even bother to show up, it wouldn't make a bit of difference. As a nation we are as broken as we ever have been. We are in distress, and the top priority in all of our lives is for the problem to be exposed, because *what you don't know* can *hurt you*. If the walls are down, if they are down in your life, your marriage, and the church of Jesus Christ, we need to find out about it. *Expose the problem.*

In order to make a difference we must:

Accept Responsibility

In verse 4 he sat down and wept.

> Verses 5-6a: I pray, Lord God of heaven, O great and awesome God, You who keep Your covenant and mercy with those who love You and observe Your commandments, please let Your ear be attentive and Your eyes open, that You may hear the prayer of Your servant which I pray before You now.

Nehemiah accepted the responsibility of a servant. He identified the problem. He sat down and wept, prayed, and fasted. He didn't criticize. He didn't condemn others, but he accepted personal responsibility. He could've become angry, asking, "Why doesn't somebody do something?"

Today, we often hear that the great need is for all

of us to become angry. "What we need is militant Christianity!" Yes, that is partly true, but Nehemiah realized what we need is not so much *anger* as we need *anguish*. The difference between anger and anguish is a broken heart. It's easy to lash out at what others do. It's easy for us to be experts in finding fault in our world and in our situation. But Nehemiah confessed, "I am not just a part of the solution, I am also part of the problem." As you read his prayer, notice that he confessed his corporate sin with the people. "*I* have sinned; *we* have sinned; *all* of us are responsible."

In our world and in our church, it is time for tears, for anguish. It's "crying time again." When you see young mothers going into those abortion clinics, does it make you weep? Does it break your heart that a million and a half babies are snatched from their mothers' wombs every year? Does that hurt you? We hear of and even sometimes experience the drug traffic and the violence. We want to get so angry, raise our fists, and yell, "Why doesn't somebody do something?" The question is, "Why don't I do something?" It ought to break our hearts. Now is not the time to point our fingers, but to fall on our knees in brokenness of prayer.

When a family breaks, does it break your heart, If I hear of another family cracking up and breaking up, I don't know what I am going to do. When a Christian leader falls, do we cry? So often, we say, "I told you so. Look what happened," criticizing and condemning rather than doing what Nehemiah did, which was to fall on his knees and face before God and pray, "Oh, God, how can I make a difference?"

He accepted responsibility. Nehemiah had all the security and authority he needed right where he was. He was comfortable and had a tremendous position. He could have stayed put. But he couldn't because God stirred his heart. It was Edmund Burke who said, "All that is necessary for the triumph of evil is for good men to do nothing." Nehemiah presented himself as God's servant and promised, "Lord, I am available to you. Here I am. I don't know what to do; I don't know how to do it, but I'm on my face before You, O God, to say I am Your servant. Do with me as You desire."

People who make a difference *expose the problem.* They are willing to ask serious questions and find out what's going on. People who make a difference are willing to *assume responsibility* and to identify with the problem. People who make a difference are willing to:

Seek the God of Heaven

Nehemiah did. He sought the God of heaven, because everything that would happen depended on God and His Word. That is why Nehemiah prayed. Nehemiah began with one presupposition, and he stated that presupposition in verse 5: "I pray, Lord God of heaven, O great and awesome God, You who keep Your covenant and mercy with those who love You and observe Your commandments." That was his presupposition. He referred to God's *character* and God's *covenant.* He confessed, "You are an awesome God. You are a great and mighty God, a faithful and forgiving God." Nehemiah was exclaiming not only, "Lord, I am available," but *"Lord, You are able."* Have you ever said that? "God, You are able. Therefore, I am available."

In the middle of crisis here was a man who believed God. Nehemiah was a realist. He understood how desperate the conditions were. While he was a realist, he wasn't a pessimist. You cannot know God and still be a pessimist because you recognize God is in control. There is the God Factor. Not long ago I read *The X Factor* by George Plimpton. The book describes the X Factor, the quality that creates excellence in the lives of people, especially great athletes. What is it about one athlete that causes him to excel above others of equal talent and equal ability? What is that extra ingredient in people's lives that comes through when the crisis and the heat are on, when the dire need is there, when the touchdown has to be scored, or the base hit is called for, or when the problem has to be solved? What is the X Factor for the Christian? It is that we have a God who can do the impossible. He is *awesome* and *able*.

Nehemiah prayed, "Oh, God, You're an awesome God. You're a faithful God." And he began to pray the Word of God. In fact, in verse 8, notice that he began reminding the Lord of His own Word. This prayer was full of Scripture. Nehemiah knew the Scriptures. He presented himself in prayer. Prayer is no substitute for work, but prayer is preparation for work. An unknown Christian expressed it, "You can do more than pray after you've prayed, but you cannot do more than pray until you pray." In prayer courage and commitment are born. Prayer inspires our vision, demands our sacrifice, stretches our faith, and increases our discipline. In the secret place of prayer, in the private place of prayer, men and women are made great by a great God.

What is the extra factor that causes some Christians to excel in their commitment and service to Jesus Christ? One devoted Christian of yesteryear explained, "Great men of God simply love God more than others." Nehemiah loved God, and it plainly shows in his prayer.

Prayer is surrender. Nehemiah was about to be committed for the task, but before he could he had to surrender himself to do the will of God. Let me remind us that prayer is adjusting our will to the will of God. We often wonder, *Why pray? If God knows what He is going to do anyway, if God already knows the answer, if God is sovereign, why pray? Why am I commanded to pray?* I believe it is because in prayer we are *exposed to the presence of God* and *experience the power of God*. It's like a photoplate. Take that photoplate into a dark place, and there is time exposure. Through the process in that dark place with time exposure, the image is formed. So it is in prayer. The more time we spend exposed in the secret place, in the quiet place, in the dark place, the more time we spend with God there, the more the image of Jesus Christ is exposed and imprinted upon our lives. So, in prayer, we report for duty, and we find out what we are to be doing.

In prayer, we surrender. It is time to put away all of our excuses and pray, "Oh, Lord, I'm yours." Nehemiah gave up his comfortable bed for a sleeping bag and a task that seemed impossible. He gave up an easy, well-paying place of honor to assume a demanding task. He gave up all of his prestige for ridicule, all of his security for danger. God was able to use a man like that and do something significant and strategic with his life, and we are still noting that today. If Nehemiah had stayed back in the palace of the king, he would have died, and no one ever would have known or heard his name. He was willing to put himself on the firing line, to expose the problem, to assume the responsibility, and to seek the favor of the God of heaven. God called him and brought glory to Himself. And in less than two months, the walls and the gates of the city of Jerusalem would be rebuilt for the glory of God! If we like Nehemiah will do the same, we too can make a difference for Jesus Christ in our generation.

2

Praying Successfully

Nehemiah 1:4-11

The theme of the Book of Nehemiah is Christian service, leadership, and commitment. It is the story of what one person who is available to God can do. *You* can make a difference. It requires only one person to make a difference in your home, in your church, in your school, at your workplace, and on your job-site. Only one person can make a genuine difference. Nehemiah did.

Where it all began was in a moment of consecration and dedication, after Nehemiah heard that the surviving children of Israel in Jerusalem were in reproach, distress, and misery. The walls were broken down. This man of God, 1,000 miles away, was swept off his feet. When he was swept off his feet, he got on his knees and began to pray. One of the tremendous recurring themes in the Book of Nehemiah is prayer.

People who make a difference are able to get ahold of God, and when God gets ahold of them, they are able to respond, move, and do His will.

How can we pray successfully, pray with power, and pray so our prayers are answered. Would you like to pray like that, so you would know that God hears you and responds to your requests?

Let us see how Nehemiah prayed beginning in verse 4:

> 4 So it was, when I heard these words, that I sat down and wept, and mourned for many days; I was fasting and praying before the God of heaven. 5 And I said, "I pray, Lord God of heaven, O great and awesome God, You who keep Your covenant and mercy with those who love You and observe Your commandments, 6 please let Your ear be attentive and Your eyes open, that You may hear the prayer of Your servant which I pray before You now, day and night, for the children of Israel Your servants, and confess the sins of the children of Israel which we have sinned against You. Both my father's house and I have sinned. 7 We have acted very corruptly against You, and have not kept the commandments, the statutes, nor the ordinances which You commanded Your servant Moses. 8 Remember, I pray, the word that You commanded Your servant Moses, saying, 'If you are unfaithful, I will scatter you among the nations, 9 but if you return to Me, and keep My commandments and do them, though some of you were cast out to the farthest part of the heavens, yet I will gather them from there, and bring them to the place which I have chosen as a dwelling for My name.' 10 Now these are Your servants and Your people, whom You have redeemed by Your great power, and by Your strong hand. 11 O Lord, I pray, please let Your ear be

attentive to the prayer of Your servant, and to the prayer of Your servants who desire to fear Your name; and let Your servant prosper this day, I pray, and grant him mercy in the sight of this man." For I was the king's cupbearer (vv. 4-11).

The bottom line of his prayer in verse 11 was that God would prosper him, God would answer his prayer, and God would give him success. An article from the *Wall Street Journal* (Monday, December 24, 1990) described executives who rely on a Very Senior Partner. The Very Senior Partner is God, and that *Wall Street Journal* article referred to successful executives who call upon God. It spoke of politicians, as in the case of Secretary of State James Baker, who acknowledge that in diplomatic power, there is always a Higher Power.

Mr. Baker was quoted as saying, "Inner security and true fulfillment come by faith. It doesn't come by wheedling power in a power-hungry town or in a town where power is king." In his own personal testimony of dependence on God, the Secretary of State testified, "I came to a place where I really needed to stop trying to play God and turn the matter over to Him." Those particular executives pointed to the impact and influence of God working in their lives in the business world, stating emphatically that worship on the weekend and business as usual the rest of the week are not "where it's at." The article concluded by stating that prayer as a management technique should not be discounted.

Indeed prayer is the world's most powerful management technique. If you want to be successful in life, learn how to pray. Nehemiah needed that confidence and reinforcement. He wanted the assurance that God would make him successful. Really, what is success? Success is knowing and doing God's will. Nehemiah, because he wanted to be successful with God, prayed. In his prayer, we learn how to pray with power and how to pray successfully.

In his prayer I want to emphasize:

The Sanctity of the Prayer

Verse 4 tells us that he heard the report, sat down, wept, and mourned for many days, fasting and praying before the God of heaven. In this prayer, he cried, "Lord of heaven, O great and awesome God." Note this reverential awe before God. He came into the presence of a mighty and majestic King. He understood where he stood in the sight of a Holy God. The Bible says, "The fear of the Lord is the beginning of knowledge" (Prov. 1:7, KJV), and Nehemiah desperately needed wisdom. In prayer he began with an acknowledgment of the awesome presence of God in his life.

When Jesus taught us to pray in the Model Prayer, he began with, "Our Father, who art in heaven, *Hallowed* be Thy Name" (Matt. 6:6, NASB, author's italics). He is an awesome, holy, and reverential God. What we believe about God will determine what we believe about prayer. If you have no faith in God, if you don't believe in God, then obviously prayer will be absolutely meaningless to you. The sad fact, though, is that many Christians, while claiming they believe in God, do not pray as if they believe in God. Sometimes we do not pray to God who is great and mighty, or somehow we think He is way off out there somewhere, out of sight, and out of mind. If only we could experience God as Nehemiah did. He came into the presence of God knowing who God is and what God can do.

That is why it is urgently vital when we pray that the sanctity of prayer be maintained. Prayer must be personal in our lives. It is essential to know that God is my Father, that I can come to Him at anytime, in any way, and in any circumstance—but casual or careless speech are not even remotely appropriate in the presence of a holy God. I believe many of us have lost the fear (the reverential awe) of God. We need to bow in the presence of One who is great and mighty. Because of Jesus Christ, we can come boldly to the throne of grace, but we are never to come brashly to that throne. Because of what Christ has done in opening the way to God, who is the Way, the Truth, and the Life, we can confidently enter into the presence of God and be certain He hears us. We are never to come presumptuously; we are never to come arrogantly, because we are in the presence of an awesome and mighty God. Nehemiah was on praying ground. His heart was prepared and cultivated through prayer, fasting, and mourning. I am impressed with the humility of this man. He understood who he was compared to the omnipotent God of glory. His was sincere, humble prayer, the petition of a man who had an intimate relationship with God.

I heard about a grandfather who was teaching his little grandson how to memorize Scripture. They came to Micah 6:8, "And what does the Lord require of you But to do justly, To love mercy, and to walk humbly with your God?" As the little fellow was trying to memorize the phrase, *walk humbly*

with thy God, he commented to his grandfather,
"Grandaddy, you know it's hard to walk humbly
when you're walking with God."

When we step into the presence of God, we must
do so in humility. Do you know why? "God resists
the proud, But gives grace to the humble" (Jas.
4:6). Can you think of anything worse than being
resisted by God? Today many are preaching a "gospel" of prideful self-love, a man-centered message.
So often we hear that all we really need is to feel our
self-worth, to love ourselves, and to assert ourselves. Thus we are inundated with the New Age
philosophy that indeed you and I are God. That
originated with Satan and was promulgated in the
Garden of Eden. The Bible tells us that every successful man or woman realizes it is not our self-
worth that matters, but our worth to God that does.
Who we are in and of ourselves is not pivotal. Who
we are in God is what counts. Nehemiah began by
falling on his face before God and humbling himself. Pride is the very antithesis of what God desires. "These six things that the Lord hates, yea
seven," . . . and pride heads the list. You cannot
pray and be prideful at the same time, because God
resists the proud. Our necessity is to confess God's
worth and our own rebellion and pride. Pride is the
mortal enemy of prayer.

In the presence of an awesome God, Nehemiah
began to confess sin. That is the actual response
of whoever goes into the presence of a Holy God.
As we read this prayer, we discover that he not
only confessed the sins of others, but he confessed
his own. He became brutally honest: "We have
sinned"—but not merely "we" but "my father's

house and I." We all have sinned. In real prayer there is no illusion or hypocrisy. Jesus hated hypocritical prayer. Some of His hardest sayings related to those religious leaders of the past who loved to pray in front of people, but their hearts were full of sin. He taught that we are not heard by our much praying or our many words, but we are heard because of a sincere heart. Nehemiah came with an open, sincere heart, and he confessed his own sin.

Martin Luther, the great Reformer, said, "Sin is contempt of God." Sin is saying, "God, I want to do what I want to do. I don't care what You think about it." When we are in the presence of a holy and awesome God, we are stricken and moved by our own sin. We admit, "It's me, it's me, it's me, Oh, Lord, standing in the need of prayer. I'm the problem, Lord. It's not my brother, not my sister, but it's *me,* Oh, Lord, standing in the need of prayer. It's not my wife, my husband, my children, my family, my country, my church. Lord, it's me. I am the one. I need You." In that moment, we reach the place of total dependence and complete openness to the Lord.

I am a man who is absolutely dependent upon the Lord God of heaven—emotionally, psychologically, physically, spiritually—however you want to describe it. I am dependent upon Him. In His presence, all my excuses vanish. All the pride is taken away because we are stripped down bare, naked before a Holy God. We can no longer alibi, "Well, Lord, that's just the way I am. I do what I do because that's just the way I am." Or, "Lord, it's not my fault. You see, it was the home I was born into; it was the family I lived in; it was the stuff I had to put up with." All the excuses disappear, and we make a clean confession, "Lord, it is me."

The sanctity of the prayer. He began by praying, "Oh, God, You are an awesome God." He had reverence. I personally believe that in our desire to help people to be familiar with God, and to know Him personally, somehow we have gone over the edge, and people are too *familiar* with a Holy God. To many He is the cosmic Santa Claus. He is "The Man Upstairs." We must return to the place where we understand Who God is with His awesomeness and greatness. We must understand that He loves us, came for us, died for us, and His grace is for us. He is a Father who forgives and befriends us when we realize what has occurred: the great God stepped down out of the glories of His heaven and came to this world to die on the cross for our sins, taking the penalty for our sins. He did not leave us broken, ruined, and desperate in our sin, but He lifted us up through Jesus Christ, His Son, and has given us eternal life.

Then let us focus on:

The Sincerity of the Prayer

Nehemiah, according to verse 4, spent months praying, fasting, and mourning. As we noted earlier, his prayer was accompanied by deep feeling, emotion, and devotion. He was bereft over those broken walls. He could never be the same. He could not turn his back. He cried. We used to hear that big boys don't cry. Here was a big man who cried and suffered.

I well remember when President Bush spoke to our denomination's annual meeting, the Southern

Baptist Convention. He described the emotional experience of deciding whether or not to pursue the war in the Persian Gulf. He described the turmoil and the tenderness of that moment and how he and Mrs. Bush prayed. As he talked about praying and preparation for "pulling the lever" and starting the war, fresh tears gushed from his eyes. Our President paused, collected himself, and continued, but he described the night in which he wept as the war was about to begin. Interestingly enough, some so-called politically astute persons observed and decried our President for that. Some asked, "Were they crocodile tears? Were they phony, political tears?" Or others suggested he should not become "so emotional." But there are many families of men and women who were in the Persian Gulf that are grateful we have had presidents who took seriously the charge of the presidency and who had compassion, even a willingness to weep, to pour out tears in the face of crisis.

Nehemiah did that. He was a prayer warrior. The Bible admonishes us to devote ourselves to prayer. Be watchful and thankful. He prayed virtually "without ceasing" (see 1 Thess. 5:17). The Bible encourages us not to lose heart in prayer but to remain persistent in prayer. Lose sleep if necessary. Don't be lazy. Don't be lukewarm. Be vigilant, be diligent. Romans 12:12 says, "Continuing instant in prayer" (KJV). As we consider our prayer lives, as I look at my own prayer life, I am asking, "Where are the tears? Where are the mourning, the persistence, and the fasting? Where are the sacrifice, the anguish, and the brokenness of our praying?" When we hear about broken walls and broken lives, we may breathe a little prayer, forget about it, and go on our merry way. Not Nehemiah—he continued in prayer.

Evangelist Jay Strack asks, "How can we go to bed dry-eyed night after night when so many people cry themselves to sleep?" When was the last time we missed a meal to pray? When was the last time we stayed up late to pray? Or arose early to call upon the God of heaven? I'm not suggesting that we have to nag God, belabor God, or haggle with God in order for Him to hear us. Oh, no. There is, though, a marvelous quality about this man's life who was willing to pound the parapets of heaven until he received the answer from God. Nehemiah was persistent, day after day, night after night.

Are we persistent in the warfare of prayer? In Ephesians 6:10-18, we are cautioned to prepare to stand against the enemy. We are to battle the wiles of the devil. We are to put on the full armor of God. We are in a pitched spiritual battle. "Praying always with all prayer and supplication in the Spirit" (Eph. 6:18a). Why? Because there is no cease-fire in this battle. We must keep on praying continually and with determination. Never give up. In every situation, pray. To pray successfully means to pray in every circumstance of your life.

Have you been in that situation, business person, when you're about to deliver a project or proposal, and you realize that you must have the strength of God, so you pause, pray, and ask God to strengthen and help you? That is an example of praying continually in every circumstance, not only praying in church but praying on the firing line. When you are having a struggle, when you are having a problem in your family, with your children, or with your life situation, do you pray? So often, we try to handle matters our own way, but when it comes down to the end, we conclude, "Oh, well, we'd better pray about it." Prayer should never be our last resort; it ought always to be our first resort, our first choice.

Nehemiah prayed with sanctity and with sincerity. The reason he could pray with sincerity is because he recognized God was awesome and was able to do exactly what he asked. *Prayer puts us in the position to receive what God desires to give.* This is the bottom-line reason for praying. Prayer has been described as "not overcoming God's reluctance but laying hold of His highest willingness to bless us." God has bounty He wants to give us. God has miracles He wants to perform in our lives, but we must place ourselves in the position to hear from Him and to realize: (1) what He wants us to do, and (2) how He wants to do it. That is what prayer is all about.

You inquire, "What can I ask God?" or "What can I talk to God about?" Ask Him whatever is on your heart, because this great and awesome God sees when the smallest sparrow falls to the ground and knows the number of hairs on your head. He is interested in everything. He is not only interested in everything, but our God can do anything. For He is "able to do exceeding abundantly above all that we ask or think" (Eph. 3:20a). What are we to ask? Why are we to ask? Because we can't "overask" God; neither can we out-imagine God. There is nothing we can ask of God that He cannot do, provided it is in His will. James says, "You have not because you ask not" (4:2).

Finally, we come to:

The Surrender of the Prayer

Nehemiah said, "I am Your servant." We should never ever ask God to do something without also asking God, "What do you want me to do?" That is what Nehemiah did. He asked God to do something, but he also volunteered, "Lord, I am willing to do something." Prayer is not an excuse for doing nothing. Prayer is *surrender, sacrifice,* and *servanthood.* David said, "God forbid that I should offer unto the Lord that which cost me nothing." Prayer is reporting for duty and being available as the servant of God.

James, the half-brother of Jesus, had deep insight into prayer. In fact, tradition has it that he was called "Old Camel Knees" at the end of his life because he had spent so much time wearing callouses on his knees. James knew how to pray, and he also knew what prayer was about. He wrote, "You have not because you ask not." He also promised, "The fervent prayer of a rightous man avails much" (Jas. 5:16). He believed in prayer, preached about prayer, and practiced prayer. But it was that same James who also wrote that if you pass someone who is hungry and you just say, "Oh, be warmed and filled. God bless you. Good-bye," there is no good in any of it. That is when he talked about faith without works being dead and futile (see James 1:17). In other words, prayer without surrender and faith without works mean nothing. We are God's means and God's method toward accomplishing His will. It is in prayer that we are enabled and energized.

In prayer we are equipped to do what God has called us to do. Never ask God to do what you are unwilling to do. Nehemiah prayed to be released by the king of Persia, Artaxerxes, specifically so he could go and serve the King of kings and the King of heaven. He did not beg over in Persia, "Oh, God, those people with their broken walls and broken lives, they're in shame and misery over there. God, send a miracle." He did not pray, "Send a miracle." He requested, "God, send me." Neither did he pray, "Oh, God, I'm 1,000 miles away. What can I do? Send somebody else. Raise up a missionary, Lord. Get somebody over in Jerusalem to feel the burden." No, he prayed, "Lord God, send me. I am Your servant."

Prayer makes us proactive. So many of us are reactive rather than proactive in life. Prayer makes us proactive. We never lack for an answer, for purpose, or for wisdom, if we spend time in prayer. Nehemiah didn't say, "Oh, Lord, I guess all I can do is pray about it. Well, at least we can pray." He didn't say, "Lord, do something over there in Jerusalem. Lord, bless all those people, comfort all of those people. Lord, send somebody to those people." He put himself at God's disposal, "Lord, I am Your servant." He, like Isaiah, said, "Here am I, Lord, send me" (see Isa. 6). Pray and obey. Mark Ephesians 3:20 again, "[Our God] is able to do exceeding abundantly above all that we ask or think according to the power that works in us." In other words,

God chooses not to work instead of us or in spite of us, but God chooses to work *in step* with us. We are colaborers with Christ.

Prayer also makes it possible for us to obey God. Yes, we are to pray for the hungry, but we are also to feed the hungry. Yes, we are to pray for the hurting, but we are also to drive to a hurting person's home, put our arms around them, and say, "I love you, and Jesus loves you. Let's talk." Yes, we are to pray for the lost. But we are to rise up from our prayers, energized by the Holy Spirit and our walk with God, and go tell the good news of Christ to a lost person. Yes, we are to go *to* God, but we are to go *for* God. And we are to wear out our knees and also the soles of our shoes. There is the surrender of prayer.

The fact is, all great men and women, like Nehemiah, are simply weak persons, not so great, until they begin to pray and discover—in the sanctity of prayer, in the sincerity of prayer, and in the surrender of prayer—the power and presence of Almighty God. That is praying successfully.

3

Stepping Up to the Plate

Nehemiah 2:1-8

1 And it came to pass in the month of Nisan, in the twentieth year of King Artaxerxes, when wine was before him, that I took the wine and gave it to the king. Now I had never been sad in his presence before. *2* Therefore the king said to me, "Why is your face sad, since you are not sick? This is nothing but sorrow of heart." Then I became dreadfully afraid, *3* and said to the king, "May the king live forever! Why should my face not be sad, when the city, the place of my fathers' tombs, lies waste, and its gates are burned with fire?" *4* Then the king said to me, "What do you request?" So I prayed to the God of heaven. *5* And I said to the king, "If it pleases the king, and if your servant has found favor in your sight, I ask that you send me to Judah, to the city of my fathers' tombs, that I may rebuild it." *6* So the king said to me (the queen also sitting beside him), "How long will your journey be? And when will you return?" So it pleased the king to send me; and I set him a time. *7* Furthermore I said to the king, "If it pleases the king, let letters be given to me for the governors of the region beyond the River, that they must permit me to pass through till I come to Judah. *8* "and a letter to Asaph the keeper of the king's forest, that he must give me timber to make beams for the gates of the citadel which pertains to the temple, for the city wall, and for the house that I will occupy." And the king granted them to me according to the good hand of my God upon me.

Never think of Nehemiah as a crusty, old prophet or preacher who has practically nothing for us today. Nehemiah was a young, energetic, dynamic leader. The lessons we learn from his personal journal called the Book of Nehemiah—his memoirs—give us many of the most incredible and outstanding examples of leadership and principles of success in all of the Bible—in fact, in all of literature. As we investigate Nehemiah, we are studying success in the service of Jesus Christ.

Over a period of time, God began to make His man. God molded and prepared him, giving His man a strategy for success in one of the most astounding and amazing feats in human history, the rebuilding of those walls. Once the construction was begun, it took only fifty-two days. What a man was Nehemiah!

Maybe you are wondering why I am using a baseball allusion for the Book of Nehemiah. I am a big baseball fan. When I was a little boy, I would play baseball in the sandlots and fields with my friends. I love the game. I will never forget the first time I stepped up to the plate in a "real" game. My dad sponsored the team so I was able to play. Ahem! We had red shirts with white letters, terrific-looking pants and shoes; I had a new glove and bat. I was seven years old but still remember stepping up to the plate in a real game. Those butterflies were flying around like buzzards in my stomach. How exciting it was finally to get into the game and off the sidelines! I had been watching some of my older friends play the game, and now I was in the game. I stepped up to the plate. What an exciting moment it was!

It was now time in Nehemiah's life after praying, fasting, and mourning to step up to the plate, to be counted, to present himself, and to enter into the game, which is what we must do. Every baseball team would love to have a player who never makes an error, who never strikes out, and who always plays perfectly. The only problem is we can't induce that guy in the stands to drop his hot dog and come out onto the field to play! In life, there are always those who criticize and minimize those who are on the field and in the action. It requires a lot of commitment to step up to the plate and to get into the game. Frankly, precious few Christians are doing it.

I recently read an article entitled "Deeply Committed Christians Less Than 10 Percent." It went, "'Fewer than 10 percent of Americans are deeply committed Christians,' pollster George Gallup, Jr., said previewing a study that will not be released until early next year." Then Mr. Gallup wrote, according to his survey, "They (the 10 percent that are committed) are more tolerant of people of diverse backgrounds. They are more involved in charitable activities. They are more involved in practical Christianity. They are absolutely committed to prayer." He also observed, "These committed Christians, though they be just 10 percent, are far happier than the rest of the population."

He continued, in summing up an analysis of his figures, "Most Americans who profess Christianity don't know the basic teachings of the faith, and they don't act significantly different from non-Christians in their daily lives. . . . Overall the Sunday School or religious education system in this country is not working. Not being grounded in the faith, the professing believers are open for anything that comes along," he warned. The study showed that "New Age beliefs, for example, are just as strong among traditionally religious people as among those who are not traditionally religious, and the churched are just as likely as the unchurched to engage in unethical behavior." The studies also revealed a growing percentage of Christians who claim they can sustain their faith without attending church.

Less than 10 percent are committed Christians, according to Gallup—less than 10 percent who, like Nehemiah, are willing to step up to the plate and declare, "Count on me, Lord. I am committed absolutely and totally to you. I want to make a difference in my generation for Jesus Christ."

I want us to address that problem and challenge you to step up to the plate. How do we do that? How did Nehemiah do it? First, people who step up to the plate and make a difference:

Pray Fervently

We have already studied Nehemiah's prayer and realize that Nehemiah mourned, fasted, and prayed. But how long did he pray? Insight is given to us in 2:1. "And it came to pass in the month of Nisan, in the twentieth year of King Artaxerxes." Let's stop right here. It was the month of Nisan in chapter 2. In 1:1 we are told it was the month of Chislev when word came to Nehemiah that the walls were down, and he began to pray. The month of Chislev is December; the month of Nisan is April. Those four months constituted concentrated, committed, fervent, and passionate prayer on the part of Nehemiah. All of that time, he waited on God and trusted Him for the moment of action. It is important for us to remember that Nehemiah didn't rush off into action or react impetuously the moment he heard there was a problem back in Jerusalem. He was aware he wasn't ready.

Before we can make a difference, we must be different. God needed time to prepare His man, so those four months were a period of prayer and preparation. Proverbs 19:2 advises that it is dangerous and sinful to rush into the unknown. The expression goes, "Fools rush in where angels fear to tread." Sometimes haste can be very dangerous unless we spend the time, count the cost, and prepare ourselves in prayer. Jesus commanded His disciples to go into all the world and preach the gospel. They didn't even know half the world existed at that time. It was a gigantic task. Jesus commissioned, "Go, you are My witnesses to the whole world." Jesus, recognizing their need for preparation, said, "But before you go, I want you to go to the city of Jerusalem and there wait until you are indued with power from on high, the power of the Holy Spirit, and then go."

God puts a premium on patience. The Great

Physician has a waiting room in which He makes
us wait, to trust in Him. It was necessary for Nehemiah to work according to God's timetable. He had
to schedule his life with God. Though there was a
delay, the delay was not a denial of his request. He
was praying day and night. Many of us would have
quit. Many feel that if they don't get an answer in
the next fifteen minutes, they figure it's not going
to happen.

Nehemiah prayed fervently and patiently. There
was a profound lesson he had to learn. That is the
door of opportunity swings on the hinges of prayer.
All real success ensues when God opens the door.
Jesus said, "Ask and it shall be given to you, seek
and you shall find, knock and it shall be opened
unto you" (Luke 11:9). Nehemiah knocked on the
door of opportunity, and when God opened that
door no one could shut it. We dare not kick down
the door and rush in until we are cognizant we are
on God's schedule. We must be in God's place at
God's pace.

In this process, this time of praying, Nehemiah
learned the most important issue one can possibly
learn about leadership. Do you know what it is? Do
you want to be a leader? Do you want God to use
you, your family, your business, your church? The
most important principle of leadership is this: in
order to lead, *you must follow*. In order to be successful, *you must be a servant*. In order to be over,
you must first be under. Nehemiah dropped to his
knees and got under. He prayed and presented himself as God's servant.

In that time of prayer God readied His man. He
died to himself. He surrendered his personal ambi-

tions. Remember, this was a man with a comfortable position, cupbearer to the king. He could have stayed right where he was, but he died to all of that. He came to the place where he was no longer interested in his security or his safety. Rather, he was only interested in serving God. Too many of us never step up to the plate because we pander to the flesh. We want to care for us first, and make sure that we're safe and comfortable before we do anything for anyone else, much less God. Jesus taught if we are going to follow Him we must die. We cannot follow the call of Christ and the cross and stay in our comfortable zone. We make so many decisions based on what is safe and secure for us rather than making decisions based on what is right and what God wants us to do. Modern American Christians are spending so much time feeding the flesh and saving their own skin rather than giving in with, "Oh, God, I want to serve You, and I know that real success is not security. Real success is not personal ambition. Real success is surrender of myself to You."

In 2:1 Nehemiah reported, "I took the wine and gave it to the king. Now I had never been sad in his presence before." Up until that time, although he had been praying and fasting, he had not revealed his sadness before the king. Nehemiah was sad that day, in a strange sense, because he had been to his own funeral. He had come to the place of death to self and death to personal ambitions. He prayed passionately and fervently. If we want to make a difference as we step up to the plate, so we must pray devotedly, passionately, and fervently. Then we are to:

Prepare Patiently

Let's look at verses 1 and 2 again:

> And it came to pass in the month of Nisan, in the twentieth year of King Artaxerxes, when wine was before him, that I took the wine and gave it to the king. Now I had never been sad in his presence before. Therefore, the king said to me, "Why is your facc sad, since you are not sick? This is nothing but sorrow of heart." Then I became dreadfully afraid (vv. 1-2).

At the prime moment, Nehemiah was in the presence of the king. Perhaps it was after dinner, and the king was perceptive that Nehemiah was upset. There was something obviously wrong, because Nehemiah had always been a positive individual. He was ever in the presence of the king, and then the king asked, "What's wrong with you? You are not sick; this must be a sorrow in your heart." What Nehemiah had been secretly hiding in his heart—the burden of the Lord in his life—ended up showing on his face. By the way, if you really have a burden for the Lord, ultimately it is going to reveal itself in some form. I like the fact that Nehemiah wasn't running around with a sour face, trying to look holy or pious. He had been praying and fasting all of those months but not in the presence of the king. He was brokenhearted, and yet he served the king faithfully. That was amazing because in only a moment he was going to ask the king for some incredible favors. What if Nehemiah had been down in the mouth, negative, and unable to do his work? When it came to that prime-time moment, when he was asking for special favors, do you think he would have had a ghost of a chance? No, he might have been dead by then, because you were never to walk around the king with a sad face, even if you were his cupbearer. There was enough bad news in the kingdom when you were a king, much less having servants around you looking like an advance agent for the undertaker. He was sad on this particular day.

Do you ever notice how people who get up at 4 or 5 in the morning to pray always tell you about it? I think if it had been me praying and fasting for four months, I'd want someone to ask, "Doesn't the pastor look burdened? Doesn't he look bad? Something must be going on. He must really be praying." Jesus taught that our praying and fasting are not to be for show. He said, "When you fast, don't be like the hypocrites who put on a sad and sour face and put ashes on themselves to be noticed and to be seen of men; but when you fast, wash your face, clean up, put on a smile, go about your business" (see Matt. 6:16, author's paraphrase). He was sincere and for real. There came the moment when he could hide his hurt no longer. What happens next shows us how Nehemiah had prepared.

Nehemiah had formulated his strategy, and God had galvanized His man during these days of prayer. God's burden had become Nehemiah's burden. God's purpose had become Nehemiah's purpose. God's plan had been delivered to Nehemiah, and he knew exactly what God wanted to do. He now had a mission from God. Do *you* have a mission from God? As a church, we have a mission statement. Your business may have a mission or a purpose statement. I want to ask you, do you personally have a mission statement? Have you ever sat down before God and, in prayer, determined what it is God wants you to do with your life? Have you prayed about your purpose, mission, and goal in life? Do you have a plan from God to ascertain how to touch as many people as possible in this generation for Christ and to affect them positively for the Lord? Do you have a plan, Dad, for your family? Do you have a plan, Mom, for your family, for your life? What about you, young people? Do you have a mission statement? Nehemiah did. It all concerned those walls.

I'm afraid so many of us have become disengaged and disenfranchised from the world. We have forgotten what it is like to be out there in the world lost without Christ. Many of us have lost our burden. We are no longer broken by the walls that are down in our society, no longer torn apart, nor do we passionately pray for people without the Lord Jesus. We're too interested in being comfortable. A great leader of World War II and the Korean War, General Douglas MacArthur, advised, "There is no security on this earth. There is only opportunity. Empty your days of the search of security and fill them with a passion for service." Are your days filled with a passion for service? Do you have an obsession to serve the King of kings and the Lord of lords? Do you have a plan of how you are going to witness for Jesus Christ to your family and your friends?

We have become very laid back about our witness in this generation. We don't want to push, offend, run anybody off, or knock anyone down. It occurred to me that as long as I have been living (forty years-plus) with as many planes as I have been on, as many athletic teams, as many events as I've attended, as many times as I've walked up and down a street, as many times as I've been in a grocery or department store, not one single person has walked up and shared Jesus Christ and the plan of salvation with me! Not one! Not many people are sharing Christ today or have a burden. Not many Christians have a passion for lost souls and broken-down walls in people's lives.

We must move out from this halfhearted effort and go to a whole-hearted effort, making a difference. Corrie ten Boom, the late Dutch author, said, "When I enter the beautiful city and the saints all around me appear, I hope that someone will tell me, 'It was you who invited me here.'" Wouldn't it be wonderful if somebody walked up to you in heaven and threw their arms around you, and exulted, "I'm here because you invited me here." That's making a difference. That's developing a burden and sharing a burden. Nehemiah prayed fervently. Nehemiah persevered patiently, and we too must:

Proceed Confidently

Now the golden moment arrived, and notice what happened beginning at the end of verse 2:

> Then I became dreadfully afraid, and said to the king, "May the king live forever! Why should my face not be sad, when the city, the place of my fathers' tombs, lies waste, and its gates are burned with fire?" and the king said to me, "What do you request?" So I prayed to the God of heaven.

This is a thrilling passage. Here he proceeded with confidence, although he was afraid and shaking, but it was the golden moment for which he had been waiting and praying. The problem is many people are never successful in life because they do not break through their fear and move on for God. Remember the parable Jesus related about the man who had only one talent. The master went away, and that servant buried his talent, rather than investing and giving his talent and serving his master with the talent.

He buried that talent, and the master returned and asked, "Why did you bury that talent?" He soon answered, "Because I was afraid." How many people never attempt great things or achieve great things for God because they are simply afraid they will not break through their fear. Nehemiah was afraid, but he prayed to the God of heaven. It was not a long prayer; it was one of those "911" prayers. The reason he could connect so quickly was because he had spent four months praying, and he had a close relationship with the God of heaven. He just breathed a prayer, saying, "Lord, this is it. It's just You and me. Now's the time. I'm going forward." And he proceeded confidently and courageously. Now look at what Nehemiah asked. The king inquired, "What do you want?"

> And I said to the king, "If it pleases the king, and if your servant has found favor in your sight, I ask that you send me to Judah, to the city of my fathers' tombs, that I may rebuild it" (v. 5).

First of all, he asked for the king's permission.

> So the king said to me (the queen also sitting beside him), "How long will your journey be? And

when will you return?" So it pleased the king to send me; and I set him a time (v. 6).

See how prepared Nehemiah was. The king threw him a little curve, asking how long he would be. Nehemiah set him a time. All during that prayer and waiting time, God showed him exactly what he needed to do and how to do it. He requested the king's *permission* and, in verse 7, the king's *protection:* "I said to the king, 'If it pleases the king, let letters be given to me for the governors of the region beyond the River, that they must permit me to pass through till I come to Judah'" (v. 7).

He was asking for a passport, for security, and safety on his journey as he moved from region to region. Not only did he ask for the king's *permission* and *protection,* but he also asked for the king's *provision.* "'And a letter to Asaph the keeper of the king's forest, that he must give me timber to make beams for the gates of the citadel which pertains to the temple, for the city wall, and for the house that I will occupy'" (v. 8).

He was so practical. He laid it out, "I am going to need timber, provisions, and other necessary materials. Please give me your help and resources, King. Give me the letter, for when I reach Asaph I will need lumber to rebuild the city of Jerusalem, the walls, and temple citadel, and my own personal residence." He sensed he was going to be there a while and would need a place to live. He had it all together. He walked right on through his fear. By faith he asked for what he needed. The king was thoroughly impressed. Have you ever noticed that people are impressed with a man who has a plan? In fact, I think the king was honored by the bold request of Nehemiah. I am convinced God is honored by our bold requests. "Thou art coming to a King, large petitions with thee bring. His grace and power are such that none could ask too much." Our King is the King of Heaven who has made all of His resources readily available to us. All of His riches in Christ Jesus are at our disposal. We can ask for our King's permission. When we go, we can freely ask for His protection and provision, and we can rest on His promise.

Nehemiah even received more than he asked for. Verse 9 reports, "Then I went to the governors in the region beyond the River, and gave them the king's letters. Now the king had sent captains of the army and horsemen with me." Isn't that just like God? Nehemiah asked for security, safety, protection, and letters, but the king sent a military escort, horsemen, and soldiers. Why? Because our God "is able to do exceeding abundantly beyond all that we ask or think" (Eph. 3:20). God always does what we ask—and then some, if we are in His will. That is what happened to Nehemiah, and that's what can happen to us. Therefore, we can proceed confidently. I confess: as many as times as I have preached and shared Christ publicly and personally, there is still not a time when I witness that I am not afraid. There are still times when I'll ring a doorbell or knock on a door, thinking to myself, *I hope they're not home*. We're all afraid. The people who do God's work and are willing to step up to the plate, even when they're afraid, courageously move through their cowardice, confident in God. It sounds contradictory, but courage is a brave way to be scared. Nehemiah was a courageous man.

One final thing, he prayed fervently, he prepared patiently, he proceeded confidently, and we too must:

Prosper Gratefully

The last portion of verse 8 sums it up, ". . . and the king granted them to me according to the good hand of my God upon me." You see who gets the credit, not the king. Nehemiah didn't give credit to himself. He wasn't breaking his arm patting himself on the back because he had been so successful. He testified, "The good hand of God was upon me." Many people think their success is personal success, and they have achieved what they have because of hard work, ability, or education. Nehemiah explained the reason for his success was because the good hand of God was upon him. Certain people sort of remind me of that woodpecker that was just about to start on a telephone pole. About that time a lightning bolt hit it and split it right down the middle. That woodpecker flew off, came back with five of his friends, and lied, "Lookie there. See what I did!" Nehemiah didn't boast, "Look what I did." He bragged on God: "Look what God did. The good hand of God was upon me." He gave God the credit. He said, "The unmistakable hand of God is upon my life." When God's hand is upon our lives, He opens the door that no one can shut.

When I came to our church, we were at a strategic point in terms of our location and our property—and where we were to go. So, we organized a "Vision 2020" committee that would study the needs of the church, the ideas of our congregation, and would seek the God of heaven to show us what we were to do. One of the big decisions was how we were going to find more space. Would we have to move? It was an issue in the church several years ago as to whether we ought to move the entire congregation to locate more land. What were we going to do?

So we began to pray, prepare, plan, and include lots of people in the surveying, but mainly we sought the face of God. The first decision we made was: God had put us here; His hand is upon us here; we are going to stay right here. But it still didn't solve the problem of space because it seemed every door was closed. We couldn't buy property anywhere around us. Five or six years ago the church tried to purchase a portion of the shopping center across the street. We offered an incredibly expensive price, and it was turned down. One more time, the door was shut in the face and in the growth of the church. Almost the very week we made the decision to stay here, God's hand was upon us here that He would provide for us here, we received information and a contact that the property across the street was available. We had no idea how we were going to buy it. Once again we began to pray and ask God for guidance, and in the whole process, there was an unbelievable series of miracles and answered prayers. Five acres-plus opened up. It is our youth center today. We are grateful for the acreage, and the property across the street is evidence that the good hand of God is upon us. God is still moving and working in people's lives who are willing to step up to the plate.

I want to give you three practical applications:

First, *prayer is a spiritual method for practical needs.* That is, God puts us into action through prayer. We learn what to do through prayer. Prayer is the lifeline of leadership. We read that in the Gallup Poll. Committed Christians pray.

Second, *we are what we are because of what we do with our opportunities.* Nehemiah had an opportunity; it was a golden moment. He was afraid, but he proceeded confidently with the plan of God, and God honored it. What are you going to do with your opportunity?

Third, *God's work never lacks for God's supply.* When God calls us, He equips us. When He charges us something, He pays the bill. When God guides, He provides.

4

The Price of Leadership

Nehemiah 2:11-20

Business persons and church leaders spend considerable time and money each year attending leadership seminars. More power to them. But did you stop to think that Nehemiah is a consummate course on leadership. It is a study on how to be a servant of Christ and how God can use you and me to make a difference for Him.

11 So I came to Jerusalem and was there three days. *12* Then I arose in the night, I and a few men with me; I told no one what my God had put in my heart to do at Jerusalem; nor was there any animal with me, except the one on which I rode. *13* And I went out by night through the Valley Gate to the Serpent Well and the Refuse Gate, and viewed the walls of Jerusalem which were broken down and its gates which were burned with fire. *14* Then I went on to the Fountain Gate and to the King's Pool, but there was no room for the animal that was under me to pass. *15* So I went up in the night by the valley, and viewed the wall; then I turned back and entered by the Valley Gate, and so returned. *16* And the officials did not know where I had gone or what I had done; I had not yet told the Jews, the priests, the nobles, the officials, or the others who did the work. *17* Then I said to them, "You see the distress that we are in, how Jerusalem lies waste, and its gates are burned with fire. Come and let us build the wall of Jerusalem, that we may no longer be a reproach." *18* And I told them of the hand of my God which had been good upon me, and also of the king's words that he had spoken to me. So they said, "Let us rise up and build." Then they set their hands to do this good work. *19* But when Sanballat the Horonite, Tobiah the Ammonite official, and Geshem the Arab heard of it, they laughed us to scorn and despised us, and said, "What is this thing that you are doing? Will you rebel against the king?" *20* So I answered them, and said to them, "The God of heaven Himself will prosper us; therefore we His servants will arise and build, but you have no heritage or right or memorial in Jerusalem" (vv. 11-20).

There is a high price for effective leadership. When many people see leaders on the platform and up front, they think how wonderful and easy that must be. But the old adage goes, "It's lonely at the top." People out front by the very nature of leadership are required to be and do this or that others may not be or do. That is the price of leadership.

It is also costly to be used of God and to be willing to be out there on the spot doing what God has called one to do. Count the cost because God is calling the entire church to servant leadership. There is a place of responsibility and accountability for every church member to exercise their spiritual gifts. Whether it is leadership up front or leadership behind the scenes, God has called the Christian to lead his family or that Sunday School class. With the call to leadership also come the price of leadership and the cost of leadership.

When Nehemiah heard that the walls of Jerusalem were down, he prayed, "God, I don't know what I can do, or what can be done, but I'm available if You call me and if You send me. I'll go and do whatever you ask." Nehemiah presented himself to the Lord in prayer. God called him and he approached King Artaxerxes to ask permission to go. The king's heart was turned by the God of heaven, and he allowed Nehemiah to go. Actually, he overturned a law he had already made when he stopped the rebuilding of the wall of Jerusalem. The rebuilding of the wall had proceeded before, and the Medes and Persians, led by Artaxerxes, stopped the project. The king changed his mind: "All right, you can go and lead in the effort to rebuild the wall." Nehemiah traveled some 1,000 miles to reach Jerusalem. He had a military escort with him sent by the king. He received more than he had asked, and yet, when he came to Jerusalem, he first went off with a few trusted advisors and friends and they inspected the broken-down walls. By himself he went by night. Verse 11 notes, "I came to Jerusalem and was there three days." For three days, he did nothing. Then on a particular night he arose and at first told no one what he was doing except what God had already been doing in his heart.

What's the cost of leadership? First, it involves:

Isolation

We think of leaders as being in the spotlight with the television cameras running and everyone observing what they are doing. Real leaders begin and continue in isolation. They practice solitude. Nehemiah secretly, covertly, under the cloak of darkness inspected the rubble. The word "viewed" in the phrase "viewed the walls" is the Hebrew meaning "to probe," as in the probing of a wound. At night Nehemiah examined the ruins, probing those gaping holes in the walls and those gates burned by fire. He was gathering his facts, but he was doing it before God alone at night. Leaders must pay the price in separation and isolation before ever going public. What happens on a platform or out front must first happen in the heart of the leader. Nehemiah had been waiting four months, praying and preparing. He was now in the Holy City. I believe the crushing reality of his responsibility to rebuild the wall and gate was now pressing him to the maximum. Now that he had seen it for himself, he needed to spend time alone with God, evaluating the situation, surveying the scene, reviewing the ruins with solitude and even loneliness. He had been called of God and committed to God. He must have been overwhelmed by the task. The sheer weight of the responsibility must have been burdensome.

There was the *dynamic of the call* and now he beheld the *depth of the challenge*. While others were sleeping, Nehemiah the leader was awake, praying, probing, studying, and surveying what

God wanted him to do. Whoever wants to be used of God as a leader must be willing to count the cost and pay the price of accountability. Leadership in serving Jesus Christ drives us to our knees in dependence upon God as we feel His powerful hand guiding us. Leaders spend time alone in *prayer, preparation,* and *planning.* They take their cues from above. Behind the scenes, in the dark, when no one else is looking but God, they determine what needs and must be done.

I've discovered this in my own life. People watch me on the platform on Sundays, but Saturdays are miserable for me. When I became a preacher of the gospel, I forever gave up having much "fun" on Saturday. I can't socialize on Saturdays; if I try, I'm no good at it. I can't enjoy recreation on Saturday, especially Saturday night. If you have ever been around me on a Saturday night, you'll wish that you weren't by the time the night is over, because the weight of the responsibility of Sunday is upon me. In the planning, praying, and preparation, I realize that I'll be standing before hundreds and even thousands of people whose souls and eternal destinies hang in the balance. I dare not come to my pulpit ill-equipped, having not paid the price in planning, praying, and preparation.

Any real leader spends time in the place of humility, far more time in the place of *humility* than in the place of *honor.* There are many people who have an impressive showcase but no backup warehouse. Have you ever met people like that? Nehemiah was a man who had plenty in the warehouse, not just in the showcase. If you are going to be a leader, it means you are going to spend more time in the prayer room than you do in the board room. If you have a place of leadership in your church—whether you teach children, young people, or adults—how can you possibly think of not preparing and offering your tip-top best in planning and paying the price? That is why we ask that our teachers work in preparation, that our choir prepare, and that all our people do the same. A leader who is worth anything to God and to the people of God spends far more time backstage than centerstage. If you fail to spend time with God backstage, you will not be worth much centerstage when you are there. Isolation is essential. Effective servant leaders used of God must go alone with Him to discover their calling and determine God's desires in view of the facts and in light of the situation. Some of you are forty, fifty, sixty years of age, or over, and have never discovered what God wants you to do with your life. In all these years you haven't spent enough time alone with God for Him to reveal what He wants to do. That is tragic.

We have many walls to rebuild in our lives, in our homes, and in our towns and cities—yes, also in the open country. Chuck Swindoll, noted author and pastor, said, "Most of us are pretty good at dressing up the outside of our lives: perfectly decorated homes, immaculately landscaped yards, polished, status-symbol cars, dress-for-success clothes, sparkling teeth. But underneath many of our manicured lives are withering souls. The polluting emphasis on empty externals and prayerless activity have produced a smog in our inner world. In underguarded moments, silence, and solitude, we can almost feel the grime the covers our real self."[1] Do you go alone with God? Do you spend time in isolation and solitude, determining what God wants to do in your life? That is the price of leadership.

Not only do we see isolation, but there is:

Identification

After Nehemiah had surveyed the ruins by night, he then approached the people with communication and identification. "Then I said to them, 'You see the distress that we are in, how Jerusalem lies waste, its gates are burned with fire. Come and let us build the wall of Jerusalem, that we may no longer be a reproach'" (v. 17). Remember the walls were down, but even in worse destitution were the people of Israel. The people were miserable, feeling hopeless, absolutely crushed and defeated. In stepped a man whom they had never met, and he challenged them, "Let's stand up. Let's rise up. Let's rebuild these walls." The people replied, "Yes, we will do it." What kind of leader was Nehemiah that the people would respond to him so enthusiastically and so readily? Any successful leader is skilled in identification and motivation. If you are a leader, you must be able to communicate, motivate, and inspire others to action—the reason being there are three kinds of people in the world. There are those who don't know what's happening. There are those who watch what's happening. There are those who *make* things happen. Nehemiah made things happen.

His first step in communicating with his people was to *identify* the problem. He was straightforward about it: "We are in deep trouble. You know

it; I know it. I've looked at these walls myself."
Sometimes the situation calls for an outsider to
come in and show us precisely what the real problem is. The Jews in Jerusalem had been walking
over these ruins for years—walking around them,
staggering through them, sloshing through the debris, the grime, the dirt, the filth, the reproach.
They had been living with it for years but doing
nothing about it. It required a man from the outside, with a vision and a heart for God, to come in
and exclaim, "*We* can't go on like this." After all, he
really was one of them, but he had been away from
his true home.

It is going to take something like that today.
What is it going to take for us to be shaken from our
lethargy as we look at the burned gates and the
ruins around us? We are in dire trouble. There is
lawlessness everywhere. Violent crime is rampag-
ing across America. Our cities have become war
zones. I'm not talking about Los Angeles or Miami.
I'm referring to Dallas, Texas. I read in the news-
paper last week that the violent crime rate in good
ole' Dallas, Bible-belt, Texas is 76 percent higher
than in New York City! Our murder rate in our city
is 34 percent higher than in "The Big Apple." This
crime and violence is senseless.

A seventy-eight-year-old lady, a leading citizen in
this city, pulled into her driveway this week and
there was accosted and attacked by a hoodlum—a
random killing for seemingly no reason. She was
gunned down in her own driveway. Police officials
report that this is happening not merely in the
crime-infested areas of our cities, but in the finest
neighborhoods. I watched on the news in horror ˌs

a twelve-year-old boy in Houston was arrested for capital murder. Beatings, shootings, knifings, stealings, and rapes are everywhere to the extent that the average citizen is living behind locked doors and security systems. The walls are down. What's going to shake us? Who can move us?

What about the financial decline of our nation? The fraud and failure of our lending institutions is costing American taxpayers billions of dollars. The national debt is beyond our imagination—not only the national debt but family and personal debt as well. People are in debt over their ears. I was watching a news report this week where college students were discussing their indebtedness with credit cards. Apparently, college students have easy access to all kinds of credit cards. Credit card companies are on campuses inviting students to enroll in their credit company. One young person had over thirty thousand dollars in debts on his credit cards! How would you like to receive that little message from your student at college? Indiscriminate buying and indebtedness amount to greed. We want what we want, and we want it right now. Gross greed is pushing us to the brink. I remember passing by one of our huge buildings here in North Dallas. It is a magnificent structure. I asked the man I was with, "What corporation's office is that?"

He said, "There's nobody in that building. It's vacant and has been since the day it was built. It is in foreclosure."

And I inquired, "What does that mean?" He went on to comment, "That building is a monument to North Dallas greed!"

We see it everywhere. People are on the verge of financial collapse because of "gimme, gimme, gimme" greed. Many Christians are so in debt that they cannot possibly pay their tithes and offerings to the Lord. If you ever reach the place where you cannot give to God, you are indeed in financial bondage.

There is also extreme immorality in this sex-saturated society. Every person determines his own morality. Evil becomes good and good becomes evil, which is an upside-down morality. Good is ridiculed, and evil is dignified. The Bible speaks of a time when our good would be evil spoken of. We are living in a moral vacuum. It used to be that we would hang our dirty laundry in the back of the house. Now all the debris, dirt, and filth are right up front, marching down the main street and on our televisions. The immorality is so obvious it is pandemic. This is resulting in the fracturing of our families. If you could only walk around the ruins with me for one week and be appalled by the ravages of family breakdowns, divorces, adulteries, pride, disintegration, child abuse, domestic violence, rapes, and abortions. Common decency and dignity are practically gone. Perhaps it is most graphic in the language we hear and that certain people use—movies, media, television, hallways at your school. It seems we have lost all sense of propriety. People will say and/or do anything publicly.

There is environmental disaster. Evangelical Christians have been absent on this issue, but we are facing ecological imbalance. We have been polluting our air, and our natural resources are being ruined. Even our drinking water and water supplies are in trouble. The ozone layer has holes in it. God has called Christians to be good stewards of the world He has given us. I think an estimated 80 percent of Americans claim that they are environmentalists or support environmental control. We Christians have been lagging behind in being a voice. We keep polluting the system and the ecological balance, and if we are not careful future generations will not be able to survive on planet earth.

There is unbridled materialism. We are living in a time when more is less. Many of us have more to live with and less to live for than any other generation. Many have expressed themselves in words like these: "If I have everything, why is it I'm so empty?" Many have more than they have ever had, and yet they are restless, empty, always on the move, and always wanting more. More, more, more! I'll never forget when one of our children at Christmas had opened up all of his presents with the wrapping everywhere—brand-new toys. We had gone to considerable expense. This child had played with them about thirty minutes and then confessed to me, "Daddy, I'm bored. I don't have anything to do." How like adults with their toys! Good grief, Charlie Brown! The difference between men and boys is just the size of the toys. One man wants his Mercedes or Jaguar—one boy wants the most complicated Nintendo. We have all of these toys, playthings, and stuff, but we're hollow! Materialism cannot satisfy.

There is a horrendous trauma of emotional and psychological breakdown today. People are living in personal pain like I have never seen. The problems people are facing are more severe and more damaging: resentment, addiction, bitterness, anger, and bitter memories of the past are keeping people in bondage. Because of the emptiness, so many are turning to New Age philosophies with all of the aberrations and the cults. All too many are even ending it all and taking their own lives. Not only do we face those problems, but we have the problem of a church that is inept, weak, and insipid. Institutional Christianity has failed. Our doctrinal and biblical integrity are lost in the malaise of relativism and modernism. We are also losing our Christian institutions to the world of secularism. While most people in America, including church members, own Bibles, only 11 percent of professing Christians consistently read their Bibles.

The walls are down. The majority don't know what they believe or why they believe. We send our students off to college and university, and they are vulnerable because we have not built walls of values and Christian ethics into their lives. They don't know what they believe or why they believe because their parents don't know what they believe or why they believe. We have not transferred our values, commitments, and beliefs. Neither have we built in protection and strength into the lives of our children. The walls are down. Nehemiah *identified the problem*. We must do the same, or our nation is doomed.

Nehemiah also *identified with the people*. He declared, "*We've* got to do something," not, "You've got to do something." He didn't say, "Get to work. I'll be in my office if you need me." A leader recognizes that he must not only identify the problem but must also identify with the people, envisioning the solutions and joining in with the solution. Not "Do what I say do," but "Do what I do. Join me. Come with me. Follow me." The apostle Paul would make statements like, "Imitate me." Paul recognized the principle of leadership: if people were to follow, he would have to set the example and the pace, and lead the way. He had to stay out front. He advised the believers, "Imitate and follow me as I follow Christ." In Bible study classes, the teachers, directors, and leaders need to be saying, "Love Christ as I love Him. Follow Christ as I have followed Him. Give of yourself, of your time, of your possessions as I give." Paul pulled no punches when he laid it on the line: "Brethren, join in following my example, and observe those who walk according to the pattern you have in us" (Phil. 3:17, NASB). Set the example. This is authentic leadership.

In verse 17, he said, in essence, "Enough of this embarrassment. The kingdom is in reproach. God's name is in disrepute." He cared more about the glory of God than personal comfort or convenience. Why do we do what we do? What constitutes the call of God to do anything? It is for His glory and a desire to glorify Him. When our churches call for workers or volunteers to serve and lead, what are we asking? "Everyone just volunteer." Not at all. We are requesting that people come before God. Let God give them a message and a mission. Let God show them what they need to be doing. Spend time alone with God and follow Him because it glorifies Him. It reproaches God when we fail in what He has called us to do.

What qualifies us for leadership is seen in verse 18. He said, "And I told them of the hand of my God which had been upon me." It was God's business, what God had called him to do. Can you point to the hand of God on your life and direct, "Follow me"? This was his resumé. He wasn't qualified because of his education or because of a diploma hanging on his office wall. I doubt if he had an office. He was qualified because he was concerned first and foremost for the glory of God. The spirit and hand of God were upon him. "Look at me, the hand of God is upon me," he testified. We follow leaders we respect. They respected Nehemiah, and therefore they followed him.

Then he continued, "The king is also supporting me." He told how God had delivered the king into his hands. First, he had spiritual qualifications, and then he presented his earthly credentials from the king. This man was credible with the people because he had a reference from God. God validated and verified His man. He credentialed him with the king because this man was faithful to the king. What if Nehemiah had not been faithful in serving the king? Would the king have recommended Nehemiah? Absolutely not. Nehemiah had spiritual qualifications. Then God used him.

The price of leadership finally is:

Confrontation

In verses 18 and 19, we encounter three men we are going to be tolerating throughout the remainder of this story: Sanballat, Tobiah, and Geshem. Immediately they began to obstruct the work of God. The moment we stand and challenge, "Let us arise and build," the devil and his crowd will yell, "Let us arise and blast." There are two kinds of people in the world. There are the obstructionists and the constructionists. Are you constructive to the work of God or obstructive to the work of God? The point is that all leaders will face the flak. All leaders will face resistance. If you determine to do anything for God, others will oppose you. There is the price of persecution. They were laughed at and mocked. Nehemiah pressed the issue, "Who are you? You don't have any part in this. The God of heaven will give us success." In other words, he was letting down the hammer: "You either get out of the way, or get on the way in the service of the Lord."

The leader must recognize that he is to accept criticism when it is valid and to be humbled by and responsive to all constructive criticism. This was not correct criticism. Nehemiah knew he had a message and mission from God. Here were these obstructionists who suddenly reared their ugly heads and tried to stop it. Nehemiah came back, "Who are you to stop this? If God be for us who can be against us?" Jesus said, "The gates of hell shall not prevail against it [the church]" (see Matt. 16:18). Theodore Roosevelt is quoted as saying, "It is not the critic that counts, not the person who points out how the strong man stumbled or where the doer of deeds could have done them better. The credit belongs to the man who is actually in the arena, whose face is marked by dust and smeared with sweat and blood—who strives valiantly, who errs and comes short again and again. There is no effort without error and shortcoming. The real leader actually tries to do the deed, expresses great enthusiasm and mighty devotion, and spends him-self in a worthy cause. At his worst, if he fails, at least he fails while daring supremely. Far better it is to dare mighty deeds and to win glorious triumphs, even though checkered by failure, than to rank with the poor spirits who neither enjoy nor suffer much because they live in the gray twilight that undergoes neither victory nor defeat."

Expect opposition and confrontation—but trust in God. If God has called you, be confident that He will see you through!

Note

1. Charles R. Swindoll, *Hand Me Another Brick* (Nash-ville: Thomas Nelson, 1990), 79.

5

Just Do It

Nehemiah 3

1 Then Eliashib the high priest rose up with his brethren the priests and built the Sheep Gate; they consecrated it and hung its doors. They built as far as the Tower of the Hundred, and consecrated it, then as far as the Tower of Hananeel. 2 Next to Eliashib the men of Jericho built. And next to them Zaccur the son of Imri built. 3 Also the sons of Hassenaah built the Fish Gate; they laid its beams and hung its doors with its bolts and bars. 4 And next to them Meremoth the son of Urijah, the son of Koz, made repairs. Next to them Meshullam the son of Berechiah, the son of Meshezabeel, made repairs. Next to them Zadok the son of Baana made repairs. 5 Next to them the Tekoites made repairs; but their nobles did not put their shoulders to the work of their Lord. 6 Moreover Jehoiada the son of Paseah and Meshullam the son of Besodeiah repaired the Old Gate; they laid its beams and hung its doors, with its bolts and bars. 7 And next to them Melatiah the Gib-

eonite, Jadon the Meronothite, the men of Gibeon and Mizpah, repaired the residence of the governor of the region beyond the River. *8* Next to him Uzziel the son of Harhaiah, one of the goldsmiths, made repairs. Also next to him Hananiah, one of the perfumers, made repairs; and they fortified Jerusalem as far as the Broad Wall. *9* And next to them Rephaiah the son of Hur, leader of half the district of Jerusalem, made repairs. *10* Next to them Jedaiah the son of Harumaph made repairs in front of his house. And next to him Hattush the son of Hashabniah made repairs. *11* Malchijah the son of Harim and Hashub the son of Pahath-Moab repaired another section, as well as the Tower of the Ovens. *12* And next to him was Shallum the son of Hallohesh, leader of half the district of Jerusalem; he and his daughters made repairs. *13* Hanun and the inhabitants of Zanoah repaired the Valley Gate. They built it, hung its doors with its bolts and bars, and repaired a thousand cubits of the wall as far as the Refuse Gate. *14* Malchijah the son of Rechab, leader of the district of Beth Haccerem, repaired the Refuse Gate; he built it and hung its doors with its bolts and bars. *15* Shallun the son of Col-Hozeh, leader of the district of Mizpah, repaired the Fountain Gate; he built it, covered it, hung its doors with its bolts and bars, and repaired the wall of the Pool of Shelah by the King's Garden, as far as the stairs that go down from the City of David. *16* After him Nehemiah the son of Azbuk, leader of half the district of Beth Zur, made repairs as far as the place in front of the tombs of David, to the man-made pool, and as far as the House of the Mighty. *17* After him the Levites, under Rehum the son of Bani, made repairs. Next to him Hashabiah, leader of half the district of Keilah, made repairs for his district. *18* After him their brethren, under Bavai the son of Henadad, leader of the other half of the district of Keilah, made repairs. *19* And next to him Ezer the son of Jeshua, the leader of Mizpah, repaired another section in front of the Ascent to the Armory at the buttress. *20* After him Baruch the son of Zabbai diligently repaired the other section, from the buttress to the door of the house of Eliashib the high priest. *21* After him Meremoth the son of Urijah, the son of Koz, repaired another section, from the door of the house of Eliashib to the end of the house of Eliashib. *22* And after him the priests, the men of the plain, made repairs. *23* After him Benjamin and Hasshub made repairs opposite their house. After them Azariah the son of Maaseiah, the son of Ananiah, made repairs by his house. *24* After him Binnui the son of Henadad repaired another section, from the house of Azariah to the buttress, even as far as the corner. *25* Palal the son of Uzai made repairs opposite the buttress, and on the tower which projects from the king's upper house that was by the court of the prison. After him Pedaiah the son of Parosh made repairs. *26* Moreover the Nethinim who dwelt in Ophel made repairs as far as the place in front of the Water Gate toward the east, and on the projecting tower. *27* After them the Tekoites repaired another section, next to the great projecting tower, and as far as the wall of Ophel. *28* Beyond the Horse Gate the priests made repairs, each in front of his own house. *29* After them Zadok the son of Immer

made repairs in front of his own house. After him
Shemaiah the son of Shechaniah, the keeper of
the East Gate, made repairs. *30* After him Hananiah the son of Shelemiah, and Hanun, the
sixth son of Zalaph, repaired another section.
After him Meshullam the son of Berechiah made
repairs in front of his dwelling. *31* After him
Malchijah, one of the goldsmiths, made repairs
as far as the house of the Nethinim and of the
merchants, in front of the Miphkad Gate, and as
far as the upper room at the corner. *32* And between the upper room at the corner, as far as the
Sheep Gate, the goldsmiths and the merchants
made repairs.

The Book of Nehemiah is multi-faceted. It is
about leadership and courage and confidence and
faith and God's will and rebuilding, but it is also
about *revival.* Specifically, it concerns leadership
in revival and how God used one man as a catalyst
to present leadership for revival. Chapter 3 looks
like one of the genealogies of the Bible. It calls
name after name, and it is the link that pulls the
rest of the book together. In fact this chapter is
really what the book is all about. The core of all
thirteen chapters and the entire strategy of Nehemiah, which he used to accomplish the rebuilding
of the wall of Jerusalem, is contained here.
   How exciting it is to realize when God is working
in your life, to know you have a reason to get up in
the morning, you have a passion and purpose for
living because you are a servant of the Lord Jesus.
You can make a difference where you are—in your
home, in your family, in your town or city, and
around the world. One person, like Nehemiah, and

others who joined Nehemiah in rebuilding the wall can make a difference together. Of course, our hero Nehemiah, faced the cold, hard facts. It was an awesome task, and it would call for more than just one of him to do it. He could not do it alone, so he challenged the people. He had come all the way from Persia, led by the hand of God.

He surveyed the scene, saw the ruins, and walked through the rubble. With every step he felt the weight of the responsibility and the heaviness of the demands on him. I believe during the midnight walk of Nehemiah 2, the strategy for rebuilding the walls developed in Nehemiah's mind and heart. He challenged the people, and they responded positively to his words and leadership. "Let us rise and build. We can't go on like this anymore. Let's do it now," he insisted. The people agreed, "We will. We will arise and build."

I've noticed in over twenty years of pastoring churches and leading congregations that people respond positively to aggressive leadership they can respect. Nehemiah was worthy of respect. He was a man of integrity. Integrity means that one is the same on the inside as one is on the outside. The people perceived in Nehemiah a person they could believe and follow. They were deeply moved, not only in their hearts, but to action. One sage put it, "Impression without expression leads to depression." They were not only *impressed* to do something, they were *moved* to do something.

Nehemiah had a plan for action. He divided segments of the wall and assigned the people a place on the wall. Each person built a part of that wall. In only fifty-two days, the wall was completed due to the cooperation of all of the people together. In this marvelous and almost miraculous story, we behold what God can do with a group of people who are willing to concur, "Let's do it."

Three principles emerging from this text tell us how to succeed today. One is:

Participation

A phrase that appears again and again in chapter 3 is the phrase *next to him.*

Verse   2:   "Next to Eliashib the men of Jericho built."
Verse   4:   "And next to them . . ."
Verse   5:   "Next to them . . ."
Verse   7:   "And next to them . . ."
Verse   8:   "Next to them . . ."
Verse   9:   "And next to them . . ."
Verse 10:   "Next to them . . ."

Do you see it? Next to them literally meant *at his hands.* We look at the involvement and participation of many people in this project. We have already seen the hand of God working and moving in Nehemiah's heart. Nehemiah had testified, "The hand of God is upon us." The hand of God was working, and now He supervised the hands of the people working. They had joined hands with God and with one another and had participated together in rebuilding the wall. The scripture teaches, "We are laborers together with God." While Christ is building the church, He is building it with our hands, our heartfelt effort, and involvement. As we concentrate on Nehemiah 3 you will discover that thirty-eight different names and forty-two different groups are recorded in this one chapter. All kinds of diverse people were involved. In verse 1, we are told the spiritual leaders, the priests, and the high priest were involved in rebuilding the sheep gate. That was important to the priest because the sheep gate was the passage into the city and into the temple where people would lead the sheep and sacrifice them to the Lord. But those priests, who were normally doing priestly duties, were out on the wall, hands on, building. When you can induce preachers to pick up a shovel, then you really are watching a miracle.

I heard about a lady who married a grocer. After her first husband died, she married a clothier. Then he died, and she married a preacher. She was asked why she married those different kinds of men.

She replied, "Well, I married the grocer so I could eat for nothing. I married the clothier so I could dress for nothing. I married the preacher so I could be good for nothing!" I'm afraid many preachers are good for nothing, but those preachers were good for something. It was hands-on labor, but they might not have had much expertise at that.

Here were preachers leading out. One principle I have always believed personally and have shared with many preachers through the years in church growth conferences and various meetings is, "Don't ever ask your people to do what you are unwilling to do yourself." So, the preachers fell in line, and in verses 9 and 12 we find that several politicians became involved. Now what a setup they had; the preachers and politicians were working on the wall. Those big shots and VIPs in the city were working!

In verse 12, we are introduced to the daughters of Shallum the son of Halohesh, the ruler of the half part of Jerusalem. That man was quite a "nabob." Some women were working on the wall, women in ministry. It wasn't common to have women out there with the men, but in this case, the women pitched in and worked on the wall. We discover in this list there were some bachelors. Therefore, there were single adults there on the wall. There were also craftsmen, those who had know-how to work with their hands and to build; on the other hand there were also perfumers and even clothiers. All of them were becoming caught up in the project.

In verse 11, we meet a fellow, Pathathmoab, who, according to Ezra 10:30, had a problem in his marriage. He broke God's laws and made a big mistake concerning his life and marriage, yet he went according to Ezra, received forgiveness, and made sacrifice unto the Lord. After his forgiveness, this man, who had basically been disciplined by the congregation and the high priest, instead of dropping out and falling away, was back on the wall, serving the Lord. That is encouraging. He didn't let the mistakes of the past keep him from doing a good work for God.

In verses 11, 19, 21, 24, 27, and 30, we see how some people worked beyond and above the normal call of duty. They did extra work. They were the kind of people who said, "Well, I've finished my part of the wall. What else can I do?" As a matter of fact, we are introduced in verse 20 to a man named

Zabbai, who carefully and earnestly repaired the other section. Nehemiah noted that this man worked earnestly. The word there means he did extra, the second mile, the baker's dozen. He did it enthusiastically. He worked hard. I like people who are not content doing as little as they can to get by. Not doing barely enough to get along and get it done and over with, but who are serving the Lord with enthusiasm. Enthusiasm means "God in us." When the Spirit of God moves, there is the fire that moves us to do above and beyond the extraordinary for Him.

Then it is recorded, tragically, in verse 5 that certain nobles from Tekoa did not put their shoulders to the work of the Lord. Isn't it interesting, in the midst of all that work, Nehemiah mentioned those who *did not* work. It was and is forever recorded in the Word of God which is living and shall never pass away: when there was a job to be done for Him, those people were absent. What a letdown! Do not let it ever be spoken of you when there was a good and great task to do for God and His kingdom that you were not involved. So many of us want to share in the victories but not the battles. Only if we share in the price of battle should we be around to share the spoils of the victory. Serving Jesus Christ should mean *all* of us participating and working. Where did we catch the idea that when we come to Christ by grace through faith, then we don't have to serve God and work hard. I think some of us have added an eleventh commandment: "Thou shall not sweat it," because not many, I'm afraid, have realized the charge to work hard to the glory of God.

He wasn't much for stirring about, it wasn't his
   desire.
No matter what others did, he was sitting by the
   fire.
The same old story day by day, he never seemed
   to tire.
While others worked to build their church, he
   was sitting by the fire.
At last he died as all must do; they say he went
   up higher.
But if he's doing what he used to do, he's sitting
   by the fire.

                                        —Author unknown

Are you sitting or are you serving? How can one
look at a blood-stained cross and glibly utter a
pseudo prayer, "Thank You, Lord, for my salvation," put his ticket to heaven in his pocket, and
never serve the Lord Jesus Christ? As long as I live,
my goal will be 100 percent participation in the
work of Jesus Christ. All of us. Why? Because people are dying without Christ. All across this city
and all across this world people are without Christ,
targeted for the judgment of God unless they respond to Christ as their Savior. We have the message of eternal life.

Perhaps we need to ask ourselves, "If every member of our church were just like me, what kind of
church would my church be?" If every person wit-
nessed like I witness, how many people would be
won to Christ? If every person attended like I attend, what would the attendance be? If every person gave like I give, what would the stewardship
be? Participation. What is the answer to a vibrant,

growing church? My answer up front every time is *people participation.*

Never give detractors an opportunity to claim you are not involved. Our purpose for living after meeting Jesus Christ is to serve Him. Don't alibi, "Well, I used to." Every church has folks who say, "I used to serve, but I'm going to let others do it now. I'm a little older now, and I've done it a long time, so I'm going to let somebody else do it." I have never read anything in the Bible about retiring from spiritual service. We are to serve Christ as long as we have life, breath, and strength. You may reply, "I'm so busy. I travel a lot." I want to challenge you: check up and consider, do you have a place on the wall? Are you participating? In view of the mercies of God, because of what Christ has done for us, we cannot help but serve. *Just do it.*

I also see emerging from this text the principle of:

Cooperation

Obviously, they participated individually, but they also participated together—teamwork. Not one of them was just alike. Some removed rubbish; some built walls and stacked bricks. Others were foreman, ad infinitum. There was wide diversity, but in the midst of the diversity, there was unity. This is a picture of how the church of Jesus Christ ought to operate. We're organized around spiritual gifts according to 1 Corinthians 12, Ephesians 4, and Romans 8. We have all been gifted from the Holy Spirit with supernatural and ministry gifts, and we are to plug into these gifts. We all make up the body of Christ. Every member is an integral part. Not all of us do the same thing. Not all of us can sing or preach or teach, but there is a ministry for every person in the fellowship of the church. Every place is pivotal.

As I have noticed in this text, not all of the people who worked were named. The heads of households and groups were singled out, but not every person had their name recorded. I thought to myself as I realized that, *I wonder how much could be accomplished for the kingdom and cause of Christ as long as nobody cared who got the credit.* It is strategic that these names were mentioned, as we'll see later, but those who weren't mentioned probably worked just as hard. Whether or not we are noticed, whether people pay attention to what we are doing, are we working to please men or to please God?

There is a fantastic text I want you to notice in Hebrews 6:10. "For God is not unjust to forget your work and labor of love which you have shown toward His name, in that you have ministered to the saints and do minister." God is not unjust. He full well knows what you are doing. Even a cup of cold water given in Jesus' name is noticed, headline news in heaven. So accept the spiritual gift, not a toy to be played with but a tool to work with, and serve Jesus Christ—with all your heart, mind, soul, and spirit. I wonder how much more we could accomplish if we all did it in that spirit. Unfortunately, in the church of Jesus Christ at-large there are too many people pulling apart and against each other.

I heard about two men who were trying to wedge a refrigerator through a door. They strained, pulled, and pushed for hours. They couldn't budge the refrigerator through the door. Finally, one of them turned to the other one and groaned, "I don't think we're ever going to get this refrigerator into this house." The other man exclaimed, "Get it into the house? I thought we were trying to get it out of the house!"

The church must move together. It's disturbing to see the foggy vision in the body of Christ neutralizing our witness. Henry Ford observed: "Coming together is a beginning. Keeping together is progress. Thinking together is unity. Working together is success." Cooperation. Hand to hand. Heart to heart. Life to life. What a fellowship that is! The greatest fellowship in the world is discovered in serving Christ together. Through our church we will be feeding the hungry and the homeless. Hundreds of our people will be involved. We will furnish blankets and food, set tables, preach the gospel, and counsel those who are downtrodden. There is no fellowship in the world like being a servant for Christ, whether it is setting up a table, serving food, or helping a elderly person off a bus. It is cooperation. In the church, there is no Lone-Ranger-type of Christianity, where each one just sort of does "their own thing." Even the Lone Ranger could depend on Tonto. But we come together for the good of all and the glory of God. Cooperation and participation.

Finally, there is:

Affirmation

Affirmation is evident in the text in that these names are mentioned. Obviously, Nehemiah had

met these people person to person, and he recorded
what they were doing. They loomed large; they
were not merely statistics. They were vital to God
and to God's man. Nehemiah assumed a personal
interest, maintaining strong interpersonal relationships. That is a requirement for real leaders.

John D. Rockefeller once remarked, "I will pay
more for the ability to get along with people than
any other ability." Nehemiah had the knack of getting along with people. He had mastered the art of
affirming them and encouraging them. Affirmation and encouragement are the key to all human
relationships.

In the best-selling book, *The Seven Habits of
Highly Effective People,* the author Stephen Covey
tells us that in all human relationships we must
put people in a win-win situation. There are four
ways to deal with people:

1. Lose-lose; In an issue, we both lose. I lose,
   you lose.
2. Lose-win; You give up your convictions and
   preferences and totally knuckle under. You
   lose and others win.
3. Win-lose; You win the battle, argument, dis-
   cussion and all the chips, and the other person loses. You put the other person in a losing
   relationship, and that is never effective.
4. Win-win; You win, I win. In all relationships,
   you seek that win-win deal.[1]

Nehemiah surely operated by the win-win principle. They all won *together* and shared the victory
together. Together! What a terrific word. Simpa-
tico. In sync. In harmony. Symphony comes from

the Greek *sumphone,* meaning working or operating together. This was also management by "walking around." He noted those who were working hard. He described and affirmed them. In reading Nehemiah's book, though, we discover that he never mentioned what he did. I like that. He did plenty around the wall. He was the kind of man who was willing to let others take the credit. He recorded their names and shared the victory and affirmation with others. He gave them a well-deserved pat on the back. "Give honor to whom honor is due," declares the Word of God.

More importantly, God did that in His Word. There is a coming judgment seat of Christ, in which every Christian servant will be evaluated and examined as to the kind of work he has done for Christ and rewarded thereby. God does not have to be reminded when we serve Him. All of the thrill is in knowing that God uses us. Can you get over the fact that God can use you, that He can take us as instruments in His hands and, as tools, build a mighty edifice for Him? He can use us as His witnesses. "I'm only one, but I am one. I cannot do everything, but I can do something. What I can do, I ought to do. What I can do and ought to do, I, by the grace of God, will do." When you do it, you can make an eternal difference. When you don't do it, you can make a terribly negative difference.

Leon Trotsky, one of the founders of Russian Communism, in 1915 was invited to Sunday School in a Chicago church. He attended, but when he arrived in his classroom, the teacher was absent and had not even bothered to replace himself with another teacher. There was no one there to share the Word of God with Trotsky. As far as is known, he never went back to Sunday School and church. I wonder what would have happened if a faithful Sunday School teacher had been present, opening the Word of God and sharing the testimony of Jesus Christ. It could have made an eternal difference.

> Only one life,
> 'Twill soon be past.
> Only what's done for Christ
> Will last.

Note

1. Stephen R. Covey, *The Seven Habits of Highly Effective People: Restoring the Character Ethic* (New York: Simon & Schuster, 1989), 218.

6

In the Middle of the Griddle

Nehemiah 4:1-9

This world is not a playground but a battle-ground! How true that is when you begin to live for Jesus Christ and serve Him. Remember that Satan, his hellish cohorts, and his unregenerate children will oppose you from the word "Go." Our job is not only to build the kingdom of God but to *battle* for the kingdom. The fact is, when God's church rises, Satan's kingdom roars.

The walls were going up around Jerusalem. Nehemiah and the people were successful as they were establishing and renewing their testimony in the city. As a result, opposition arose. Inevitably, opposition will come against us when we attempt a work for God. Where there is building, there will be battling. Where there are friends, there will also be foes. There is progress, and progress means movement, and movement means friction.

D. L. Moody, the remarkable evangelist of the nineteenth century, quipped, "The devil never kicks a dead horse." Anywhere and anytime that

God is glorified and Jesus Christ is magnified, you can count on the fact that the devil and his disciples will go to work. That is what happened in Nehemiah 4.

1 But it so happened, when Sanballat heard that we were rebuilding the wall, that he was furious and very indignant, and mocked the Jews.   *2* And he spoke before his brethren and the army of Samaria, and said, "What are these feeble Jews doing? Will they fortify themselves? Will they offer sacrifices? Will they complete it in a day? Will they revive the stones from the heaps of rubbish—stones that are burned?"   *3* Now Tobiah the Ammonite was beside him, and he said, "Whatever they build, if even a fox goes up on it, he will break down their stone wall."   *4* Hear, O our God, for we are despised; turn their reproach on their own heads, and give them as plunder to a land of captivity!   *5* Do not cover their iniquity, and do not let their sin be blotted out from before You; for they have provoked You to anger before the builders.   *6* So we built the wall, and the entire wall was joined together up to half its height, for the people had a mind to work.   *7* Now it happened, when Sanballat, Tobiah, the Arabs, the Ammonites, and the Ashdodites heard that the walls of Jerusalem were being restored and the gaps were beginning to be closed, that they became very angry,   *8* and all of them conspired together to come and attack Jerusalem and create confusion.   *9* Nevertheless we made our prayer to our God, and because of them we set a watch against them day and night (vv. 1-9).

Here we plainly view the strategies of Satan and those who oppose the work of Jesus Christ. It hap-

pens again and again and over and over even today.
The method of operation, the strategy, and the
techniques Satan used then he also employs today
to keep us as believers from growing in Christ and
building our lives to the glory of God. The devil's
goal is to keep the people of God from advancing,
achieving, and attempting great tasks for Him.
The first of these strategies is what I call:

Derision

Ridicule, mocking, laughter. When Sanballat
heard, he was indignantly angry and responded by
deriding and scornfully accusing the people of
God. He was calling them names and referring to
them as feeble, "pitiful." Of course, such actions
are infantile. Yet, it has a powerful effect at times.
The devil loves to insult God's work, God's Word,
and God's workers. We must be extra careful when
the enemies of faith are advertising and pushing
our own work. The fact is: everytime I see in the
Bible where a tremendous work for God is happening, the devil is against it! Somehow, we have concocted the idea that the gospel must appeal to
everyone and please everyone, including the world
that does not believe. Ridiculous!

Billy Graham's new book, *Hope for the Troubled
Heart,* is one of his best. He writes "In some
churches and radio and television programs, we
see an effort to make Christianity popular and
always positive. This may be a comfortable cush-
ion for those who find the hard facts too difficult.
Within the New Testament, there is no indication
that Christians should be healthy, wealthy, and
successful in this present age."[1]

He continues, "Many in Christian television, radio programs and churches have been geared to please, to entertain and gain the favor of this world." Then he concludes, "The temptation is to compromise, to make the gospel more appealing and more attractive."[2]

I can guarantee you that temptation is always on any preacher of the gospel. Everytime I stand before a magnificent congregation like ours, and realize there are all kinds of people looking on with all kinds of persuasions and opinions, it can become tempting, in trying to please and reach people for Christ, or to soften the impact of the gospel message. But we dare not compromise the truth of the Word of God! Some may laugh because the gospel is an offense to those who do not believe.

When Jesus began His teaching and healing ministry, many flocked after Him to enjoy the good meals at the feeding of the 5,000, and on other miraculous occasions they enjoyed the crowds and the popularity of our Lord—then He began to speak of death and following Him and the cross. When He did that, hundreds, and even thousands, of them disappeared. Jesus talked about discipleship and picking up the cross. He spoke of counting the cost. As I read my Bible, I discover that every person in the Bible who did anything for God was ridiculed, mocked, or opposed.

I remember David, the shepherd boy, who came out against the giant, Goliath, who sarcastically criticized David and the children of Israel, even as Nehemiah was criticized here. David stood tall and strong and killed the giant. He refused to let the mocking and laughter keep him from doing the will of God.

Our Lord Jesus Christ experienced mocking and scourging and beating and ridicule and laughter and derision and false accusation—name-calling on one occasion when Jesus spoke of His Deity and of the salvation He offers. The Pharisees jeered, "We were not born of fornication." They were slandering the purity of the Lord Jesus to somehow suggest that He was not the virgin-born Son of God, but an offspring born out of wedlock in an illegitimate relationship. Our Lord experienced the sting of sarcasm and the mocking of men. Some of the very members of the crowd, when he rode into Jerusalem on that donkey, who enthusiastically yelled, "Hail Him, Hail Him!" ultimately screamed, "Nail Him. Nail Him to the cross!" when He stood before Pontius Pilate.

Derision will follow you if you make a consistent stand for that which is good and righteous. You'll be the "odd man out." You'll be a "Jesus freak," a fanatic.

We are encountering life-and-death struggles on moral and ethical issues facing our nation. Yes, sexual harassment is bad. It is a sin and a crime. We hear about it every day of the week. As this goes to press Mike Tyson, the former heavyweight boxing champion, has been convicted of rape. The AIDS virus is a horrendous plague. It is estimated that by 2000 A.D. there will be perhaps 100 million cases of AIDS and/or the HIV Virus in the world—and those will be the reported cases.

One of the main issues on the table right now is

Roe vs. Wade. Many politicians are criticized if they take a pro-life, anti-abortion stand. Vehement national organizations are for so-called abortion "rights," while thousands of pro-life, anti-abortion advocates have been arrested simply because they demonstrated outside of abortion clinics. Pro-abortionists continue promoting and abetting the murder of unborn babies. Media and movie stars crusade for saving the seals and the rain forests, and yet some of those same celebrities will demonstrate for those who want to snuff out babies in their mothers' wombs. Does that make sense? To many the snail darter fish in East Tennessee waters is more important than a living child created in the image of God. This nation has lost its way in the darkness.

In addition, recent spectacles in our nation's capital are absolutely appalling. Our eyes and ears were assaulted by the Clarence Thomas-Anita Hill hearing before the United States Senate. Interest groups of all kinds ransacked Judge Thomas's garage for dirt from his past. Legal experts, special-interest groups, politicians, and the press sought to disqualify Thomas merely because they were afraid that he would help swing the court in a more conservative direction. Thomas was confirmed but not without embarrassment to the entire world. We used to say, "Sticks and stones may break my bones, but names will never hurt me." Judge Thomas put it like this: "I would rather take an assassin's bullet than this process." These kinds of proceedings are a disgrace to the body politic.

"And the beat goes on . . ." The funeral dirge of America.

Anytime you take a stand for righteousness and truth, you can expect opposition and ridicule. It happens every day when you decide to speak out for Christ. Here is a student who determines, "I'm not going to participate in the drunkenness on my campus. I'm not going to participate in the immorality here. I must stand for Christ." What is he called? "Wimp." "What's wrong with you?" "What, are you better than we are?" The laughter. The mockery. The derision.

It may be that in your own home you have to stand alone for Jesus. You want to sell out and live for Christ, but in your own home you may be called a fanatic or a fool. Take a stand for the Word of God, its truth, its validity, its inerrancy, and some will mock you for that.

Many people would rather not face the issues and the facts but instead engage in name calling, slander, and innuendo. It is terrible to ridicule.

Nehemiah's people and project were scorned because the enemy is the great destroyer. Jesus is the builder, but Satan will tell you it is impossible to rebuild your home, your marriage, your life. I am proud of many professional athletes who are taking a stand on their teams by having chapels and outstanding Christian organization where teammates are praying and studying the Bible together. Have you noticed after many professional football games today that several of the players from both teams are kneeling in the middle of the field and praying together? It is a beautiful sight. But I was watching one of the late-night talk shows, and they were ridiculing and bringing "experts" and lawyers to point out how wrong, how discriminatory, and how exclusive that was for those players to be on the field praying or having chapel. Daryl Strawberry, the Dodger, and brand-new Christian, was having it tough the first part of the 1991 season. He wasn't hitting, and do you know what those "experts" claimed? "Well, it's because he's become a Christian. He's lost all of his fire and competitive edge. He's a lousy player now because he's a Christian. He's wimping out." The second half of the season, he tore the league up. I didn't hear any of those people say, "Well, it's because he's a Christian that he's tearing the league up, hitting .300, and driving in those runs."

What did Nehemiah do? Read it for yourself. He prayed, "Hear, O our God, for we are despised; turn their reproach on their own heads" (v. 4). That is a remarkable phrase. Turn their reproach, ridicule, and criticism back on their own heads.

Guess what Nehemiah prayed about those who were trying to destroy the work of God? "God, sic them! Go get them, God!" "Vengeance is Mine," says the Lord (see Deut. 32:35; Heb. 10:30). Nehemiah's "sic-'em" supplication was strange. Someone might look at that and say, "That is a subChristian prayer"—praying that God would turn their wrath back on their own heads, that God would not even forgive their iniquity! Nehemiah realized the seriousness of the situation and that sin is a reproach. The exposure of sin and rebellion offends many. He carried it to the Lord in prayer, resting in the call of God upon his life. He knew he had the people with him, for him. He rested in that perspective, and then he prayed against those enemies of the people of God and the work of God.

Those people were murderers, haters of God, and they would have destroyed the work of God. We are too often complacent about the enemy. Holy anger ought to burn against sin, and a boldness for the work and Word of God should glorify His name. If you are scorned and ridiculed, if the work of God is mocked, you pray. Keep your knees on the floor and your nose in the Book and your eyes on the Lord— and don't be detoured or slowed down. Stay off the side streets. Nehemiah wrote, "The people had a mind to work" (v. 6). They overcame the derision.

Second, there came:

Distraction

Verse 7: "Now it happened, when Sanballat, Tobiah, the Arabs, the Ammonites, and the Ashdodites heard that the walls of Jerusalem were being restored and the gaps were beginning to be closed, that they became very angry." Again, anger was being spilled there. All of those ruffians conspired together to attack Jerusalem and create confusion, division, and distraction. They came with force against the people of God. Satan is a lion seeking whom he may devour. Notice that the number of the enemy was multiplied. In chapter 2:10 it was just two that opposed the work. In chapter 2:17 there were three. In 4:7 there was a multitude, a full-blown conspiracy as the enemy rallied its forces. They surrounded Jerusalem. The situation seemed hopeless, hopeless except for the fact that while the enemy could surround the city, they could not build a roof over the city to keep the people of God from looking up. The people put their eyes on the Lord!

Notice what Nehemiah did in verse 9: "Nevertheless, we made our prayer to our God, and because of them we set a watch against them day and night." Don't you love this? They prayed, realizing their strength and source was in God. They also understood what it meant to watch and pray. Nehemiah not only prayed, but he set a watch, that is, he posted guards all around the city. Ultimately, he put a sword in the hand of the workmen. They had a trowel in one hand and a sword in the other, both building and battling. Nehemiah armed and prepared the people. If you are going to build you must be prepared to battle the opposition. We must be willing to defend what we build. We must be willing to believe, battle, and build.

There are so many people who want to battle all the time, always looking for a fight, crusading constantly against this or that. Some are known more for what they are against instead of what they are for. Always battling, they never build anything as a result. David was not allowed to build the temple. Do you remember why not? It was because the Scripture declares he was a man of war. Because his life was filled with war, and he was constantly on the battlefield, it wasn't his call to build the temple. A man of war. We must guard against always battling and never building, but by the same token, we must also be careful because there are some who only build and never defend what they build. They build great churches or great institutions, and then are unwilling to battle and to stand for what is dedicated to the glory of God.

Reggie White is one of the best football players in

the National Football League. He is a defensive end for the Philadelphia Eagles. Reggie is known as the "Minister of Defense." He's the Reverend Reggie White, a preacher of the gospel. During one particular game, Reggie was beating his blocker continually. The ball would be snapped. Reggie would evade his blocker, and sack the quarterback. Next play, he made an inside move. The quarterback was down again. He defeated his blocker. The next time Reggie knocked down his blocker and took the quarterback down. Reggie came back to where his blocker was getting up, and Reggie, like a Christian, put his hand down and helped him up. He said to his blocker, "Jesus loves you, and I love you, but you better learn how to block!"

God's people had better learn how to block and defend what God has led them to build. We must constantly be on guard against those who would try to destroy what God has done. So, Nehemiah kept the people working. The devil will do all he can to stop the work with derision and ridicule; and if that doesn't work, he will try distraction and confusion. The people of God must stay with the work.

Therefore, my beloved brethren, be ye steadfast, unmoveable, always abounding in the work of the Lord, forasmuch as ye know that your labor is not in vain in the Lord (1 Cor. 15:58, KJV).

And let us not be weary in well doing: for in due season we shall reap, if we faint not (Gal. 6:9, KJV).

If God be for us, who can be against us? (Rom. 8:31b).

Stand up, Christian. Keep your place on the wall. Don't allow the devil's distractions, ridicule, laughter, or mocking crowd to keep you from being his man and woman in this generation.

Jesus had a message for us when we are mocked. "Blessed are you if men should revile you and persecute you and say all manner of evil against you falsely for my sake, for great is your reward in heaven."

Far better than the applause of man and of this world are the words of the Lord, "Well done, good and faithful servant."

Notes

1. Billy Graham, *Hope for the Troubled Heart* (Dallas: Word Publishers, 1991), 36.
2. Ibid., 39.

7

Defeating Discouragement

Nehemiah 4:10-15

10 Then Judah said, "The strength of the laborers is failing, and there is so much rubbish that we are not able to build the wall." *11* And our adversaries said, "They will neither know nor see anything, till we come into their midst and kill them and cause the work to cease." *12* So it was, when the Jews who dwelt near them came, that they told us ten times, "From whatever place you turn, they will be upon us." *13* Therefore I positioned men behind the lower parts of the wall, at the openings; and I set the people according to their families, with their swords, their spears, and their bows. *14* And I looked, and arose and said to the nobles, to the leaders, and to the rest of the people, "Do not be afraid of them. Remember the Lord, great and awesome, and fight for your brethren, your sons, your daughters, your wives, and your houses." *15* And it happened, when our enemies heard that it was known to us, and that God had brought their counsel to nothing, that all of us returned to the wall, everyone to his work (vv. 10-15).

"Discouragement is the chief occupational hazard of being a Christian," an anonymous believer suggested. Discouragement is a powerful tool the enemy, Satan, uses against us.

An old story has it that hell's denizens were having an auction down there. Satan had to reduce his arsenal, so the hellions were auctioning some of their weapons. The one auctioned off at the highest price was the tool of discouragement! Only a story but it packs a wallop . . .

Have you ever been discouraged? Sure, we have all been discouraged. It can range from the "moody blues" all the way to severe clinical depression and all that is in between. Discouragement can attack us even when we are walking with God.

Somehow we may think discouragement hits us only when we don't have our lives together, but some of the greatest saints of all time have been discouraged. Some of the great biblical heroes like Moses, Elijah, Jeremiah, Jonah, David, Simon Peter, and others have been deeply discouraged, despairing, and depressed. Discouragement can also pass through all kinds of phases. As I was thinking of the phases of discouragement and depression, I listed them.

One is *listlessness*. It is that feeling of the blahs. Then, if we don't deal with it, it moves to *sadness,* an overall weariness. Then it goes to the feeling that *nothing matters,* nothing makes a difference. Then comes *helplessness,* feeling caught and chained by the discouragement or defeat. Next is *hopelessness,* feeling that there is no hope. We can live without money and a while without food or water, but we cannot really live a day without hope.

That sense of hopelessness transfers down to the feeling that *nothing is ever going to change.* Nothing is going to improve. Then it shifts over to the idea that *no one cares.* "No one cares about me or about my problems. No one understands what I am going through." If you don't deal with it at that point, it merges into *anger* and a *sense of rejection, resentment,* and *bitterness.* Then there is the final stage which is the feeling that "I want to die. I don't want to go on. I just want to quit. Stop this world, I want to get off." Multitudes of people are facing discouragement today. Some of you have a heavy heart and a broken spirit. You need encouragement from the Lord.

What happened to the children of Israel in their discouragement and subsequent encouragement can happen to you. By the power of Jesus Christ you can defeat discouragement. In order to defeat discouragement, perhaps we need to understand what causes it. The causes of discouragement are delineated in the Word of God. The Word of God is so practical and personal to us. There are five reasons for discouragement found in our text.

The first cause is:

Fatigue

Verse 10: "Then Judah said, 'The strength of the laborers is failing.'" They had been working on this wall and now they were dead tired, worn out. Physical depletion and fatigue were setting in. Certainly this is a cause for disappointment and discouragement today. You have been pushing it to the limit. Perhaps you are a workaholic. The hours have been mounting up and you are physically tired. The pressure and stress of your job or the responsibilities of your life are getting you down. Many of you ladies have the responsibility of not only carrying a job, working 8-5 or beyond, and also the responsibility of the children and the home, and you are absolutely ready to collapse. When we are tired and our nerves are jangled, when we are distressed and not getting the proper nutrition or rest, we are prime candidates for discouragement and depression to set in. Fatigue. Weariness. We become weary in the battle.

The second cause is:

Frustration

Verse 10 also says, "There is so much rubbish that we are not able to build the wall." They were frustrated. All the rubbish was around them—the trash, the clutter, the debris. They had lost sight of their goal, and they had lost confidence in themselves. Their vision was gone. They were thinking, *there is too much to do.* They were frustrated with the mountains of rubbish that stood before them. That can happen to us and lead to depression. In this case, the problem was that the attack came from the inside. Notice it was the tribe of Judah (v. 10) who complained. It was the strongest of the tribes of Israel. This would be like your strongest leader becoming frustrated and then facing internal accusation. At first these accusations came against them from Tobiah, Sanballat, and Geshem—from the outside. They were enemies from without.

Sometimes we can handle the enemies from without better than the enemies from within.

Sometimes we were counting on people, trusting in them, and looking to them for leadership and guidance, and then suddenly they moaned, "Oh, we're discouraged. We can't do it. We can't go on." There is frustration because they were halfway through in the project, and that becomes one of the most critical times in any project or point in your life—when you are about halfway there.

It is like a person suggesting, "Let's climb that mountain over there."

You ask, "How long is it going to take us?"

And they say, "Oh, it will take about forty-five minutes to get to the top." About forty-five minutes later, when you are struggling and sweating to reach the top, you turn around to your friend and ask, "How much farther is it?" He says, "We're about halfway."

And you respond, "Wouldn't the view be just as good here as right there at the top?"

Or it is one of those "honey-do" days, guys, and your wife purrs, "Honey, would you paint the garage?"

You reply, "Sure I would. That won't take long. I can get it done in a hurry."

You go out, grab paint and a brush, and start painting the garage. You have been painting about two hours, and a ball game is on, but you are still out there making a mess. Your wife brings you a cool glass of lemonade. You inquire, "Honey, am I about through?"

She says, "Looks like you're about half through." Man, that's tough!

Frustration. On a more serious level, there are times when we are frustrated, and it seems we will never make it, we are never going to win, or reach our destination. Depression and discouragement can set it.

A third cause is:

Faultfinders

We have already met Sanballat, Tobiah, and Geshem and all of their fellow faultfinders. Now comes Judah from within, and the criticism falls. "There is so much rubbish, and we are not able to do it." The faultfinders. Criticism and cynicism can be dreadfully defeating. Even at this moment someone may be saying things that are hurting you, and it is "eating you alive." Carping critics are everywhere. If you listen to the faultfinders and the negative voices, it will keep discouragement in your life.

Fourth, there is:

Failure

"There is so much rubbish that we are not able to build the wall" (v. 10). What was this rubbish? It was the remains and garbage from the past, the broken-down rocks, cement, birdgates, and that debris all around them. They were trying to build through the rubbish. They complained there was so much rubbish they were unable to build the wall. The rubbish was a constant reminder of past failures. They were looking at the debris, and we must realize that debris and discouragement are ugly twins. If you become caught up in the garbage of the past, you will never move forward today.

There was failure. They cried, "We can't do it." They lost their confidence and felt inadequate.

"We're not able. Look at all this mess." Maybe you are looking at your own life and trying to build it for good and for God. You are thinking, *My health is failing. What am I going to do?* or *My marriage has failed.* What about the debris, remains, and reminders of the past? Or maybe your career is failing. All of those dreams and aspirations have disappeared. Some of you men are at midlife; the wall is half-built. You are not where you want to be, and you are discouraged. Perhaps your career and financial situation have collapsed. Maybe your children have let you down.

I suppose there is nothing more damaging to the heart and life of a parent than for a child to reject the parent and/or their values, or for those children somehow to disappoint you. Maybe emotionally you have failed. You just can't get on top of your life, and all kinds of struggles are churning emotionally. Perhaps your faith has diminished. You came to Christ with every intention of living for Him and experiencing the fullness of the Christian life, with all it means, and to bask in all of those promises, but your faith has diminished. Maybe you have failed God, and you feel so badly about it. You look inward and sigh, "I don't even know if I can go on anymore. Look at all of this mess. Look at all of this trash." Discouragement attacks.

The fifth cause is:

Fear

Verse 11 says, "Our adversaries said, 'They will neither know nor see anything, till we come unto their midst and kill them and cause the work to cease.'" That will grab your attention. Fear. The fear of death. The fear of failure. The fear of rejection. This conspiracy was against them. Do you know why they were living in such torment and fear? The key is seen in verse 12, "So it was, when the Jews who dwelt near them came, that they told us ten times, 'From whatever place you turn, they will be upon us.'" The Jews who lived near them gave the fearful report.

What does that say to us today? Anytime you study your Bible, you need to ask, "What did it mean then and today what does it mean to me personally?" They lived too near the enemy. These Jews came and gave this fearful report. They had been living close to the enemy. If we listen to the fearful voices of the world, we will be afraid constantly. Many people are terrified. This is not of God. The Spirit of the Lord has given us a spirit of "power, love, and a sound mind" (1 Tim. 1:7). We should not fear, but if we listen to the world and get too close to the enemy, confusion and cowardice will set in. Of course, the problem with discouragement and depression is that they are so contagious and infectious. Nehemiah rushed to take immediate action before it spread like a cancer throughout the entire camp of Israel. The building project would be defeated without quick, decisive leadership. Nehemiah gives us the cure just as he gave the people the cure. You might remark, "You're talking to me today. I'm down, worn out and discouraged. I'm ready to quit. What do I do about?" Nehemiah tells us precisely what to do about it.

First off, he tells us (v. 14) to:

Remember the Lord

He gathered the people together and challenged them, "Do not be afraid of them. Remember the Lord, great and awesome." What was Nehemiah communicating? "Time out." He called them off of the wall and out of the work, rallied them together, and said, "Wait a minute. We need to huddle up." How many football games have you seen lost at the last minute because the coach didn't properly use his time outs? Nehemiah realized it was time to huddle. When he called the people together, they were tired. "Look," he announced, "remember the Lord. Put your perspective back in focus. Remember a great and awesome God. Look at Him. Listen to Him."

There have been times in my life I have been down and discouraged, when God Almighty has absolutely carried me through. He will carry you, too, and give you supernatural strength, even in the middle of dark days and nights. At other times He will give you blessings that will help you, like His Word or prayer, because He cares. The Bible makes it manifestly clear that Jesus has borne our griefs and carried our sorrows. I would suggest Isaiah 53 as a reminder at least once a week. The Savior knows how you feel and when you hurt. He will share that sorrow and hurt with you.

So, there are times when we must withdraw for prayer, Scripture, and rest. Jesus said, "Come unto me, all ye that labor and are heavy ladened, and I will give you rest" (Matt. 11:28). There was a time when David, the psalmist-king of Israel, was weary and worn, ready to quit. Yet, the Bible says that David encouraged himself in the Lord (1 Sam. 30:6). When you are discouraged, find your encouragement in the Lord. David later exulted in the Psalms, "I keep the Lord always before me. Because He is at my right hand, I shall not be moved." "I shall not be moved" appears four times in the Psalms. I call on you to receive Jesus as your Savior, before the tough times and before you are despondent, discouraged, and in turmoil, because it will happen. How can people face the tragedies and tribulations of life without knowing Jesus Christ? Remember the Lord, remove your eyes from your problems, pains, and rubbish. Put your eyes on the Rock, the Lord Jesus Christ. You will not be moved if you are on the Rock.

Dave Drevecky, a splendid Christian and former All-Star baseball pitcher for the San Francisco Giants, discovered a tumor in his pitching arm. The growth was cancerous, and the surgeons ended up removing 50 percent of the muscle in his pitching arm. It seemed his career was over. Yet, he worked with that arm, and through prayer and rehabilitation, he came back to pitch again and defeated the Cincinnati Reds 4-3 about a year later. It was an awesome moment. People mobbed him, but Drevecky gave God the glory. He testified, "It's a miracle." When his turn came next time, he threw a fast ball, and when he did, the bone in his left arm snapped. Drevecky reported that it was like having his arm cut off with a hatchet. He collapsed to the ground and was carried off the field. Though he tried to rehabilitate the arm one more time, it was impossible to do so. Eventually, Dave's left arm and shoulder had to be amputated, yet his faith is strong and growing. In his book, *Comeback*, Dave Drevecky wrote, "Nobody ever promised that life would be fair. Everybody is going to have adversity. The only way to handle it is to take our eyes off our circumstances and put them on the Lord."[1] Remember the Lord.

Second, *get together with family and friends.* This is thoroughly practical. Verse 13: "Therefore I positioned men behind the lower parts of the wall, at the openings; and I set the people according to their families, with their swords, their spears, and their bows." You can read it here how he closed in the ranks, how he drew people together. He put families with families and friends with friends. When you are discouraged, if at all possible, you need to find families and friends to encourage you. That is why we must have leaders like Nehemiah to inspire us, motivate us, and challenge us to stay in the battle.

We need friends who are energizers, enablers, and encouragers. If you have the blahs or are seriously depressed, you have need of rallying with God's people. Get with a Christian friend, a brother or sister in Christ who loves you and cares about you. Open up and share your heart, praying together. That is why it is urgent to have Christian friends we find at church, because in the fellowship of God's people are people of faith who have the answers, who know how to pray and love unconditionally, and can put a warm arm around you and hold you close. We need the Lord, but we also need one another.

It is like the little girl who was afraid in her bedroom. It was so dark, and her daddy went in and asked, "Honey, why are you crying?"

"Because I'm so alone."

"Well, you have your teddy bear. Hug your teddy bear."

"I don't want my teddy bear. I want someone with skin on it!"

We need someone with skin, flesh, and blood to come and put a loving, warmhearted hug around us and lift us up. The Bible says, "A brother is born for adversity." That is what brothers and sisters are for. My favorite definition of friendship is: "A friend is someone who comes in when all the world goes out." So, we need to gather with friends and encourage one another. Everyone needs grace, mercy, love, kindness, and encouragement. Not only do we need friends like that, but we need to be a friend like that.

Third, *prepare for the future*. Take a forward look. They did that in verse 15, "And it happened, when our enemies heard that it was known to us, and that God had brought their counsel to nothing, that all of us returned to the wall, everyone to his work." Have you ever noticed that most of the 1,001 things we worry about, God ends up bringing to nought? Then we wonder, *Why did I ever worry about that?* God handled their situation, and everyone of them returned to work. In other words, prepare for the future. If you are discouraged today, God may be preparing to do a great work in your future. This may be a down time preparing you for an up time. The valleys lead to the mountaintops. Defeats are but harbingers of victories to come. Out of the weakness of our life we can find strength to grow.

Have you thought about the fact that some of the greatest poetry, music, and testimonies for Christ have emerged from crisis and periods of disillusionment and discouragement? If you are discouraged, prepare for the future. Expect a blessing. Don't quit because the blessing may be waiting around the corner.

Fourth, *be productive.* "And I looked, and arose and said to the nobles, of the leaders, and to the rest of the people, 'Do not be afraid of them. Remember the Lord, great and awesome, and fight for your brethren, your sons, your daughters, your wives, and your houses'" (v. 14). Resist the enemy, and he will flee from you. Discouragement is addictive. If we become discouraged, it is a downward spiral, and we turn increasingly inward and negative. It can become worse and worse. Those kinds of feelings feed on one another. Ultimately, we are wallowing around in self-pity, stuck and can't get out. That is when we are inclined to throw a pity party. The problem with a pity party is that nobody wants to show up.

We can become overly introverted, thinking only of ourselves. The cure is to turn outside of ourselves. If you are hurting, help someone else. Be productive. That is why Nehemiah urged the Jews to fight for their friends and family. People are counting on you. You may not think so, but you can make a difference. People need you. They are relying on you to stay faithful and strong. Don't quit. Get back into the battle. That is why your faith in Christ is so vital. It is a can-do faith. "I can do all things through Christ who strengthens me" (Phil. 4:13). Christ not only transforms our spirit, but He transforms our way of thinking and looking at life.

While there are times when we are discouraged and down, God's Word promises us that we can defeat discouragement through the victory which is ours in Jesus Christ. I don't know how anybody faces life without Christ. Religion will not do it, but only the reality of having Christ as Lord and Savior of your life.

Note

1. Dave Dravecky, *Comeback* (Grand Rapids, MI: Zondervan Press, 1990), 79.

8

A Question of Character

Nehemiah 5:1-13

A startling new book on the life of John F. Kennedy is entitled *A Question of Character.* The author believes the national perspective of the former president is sadly mistaken. While many believe Kennedy to have been a young, healthy, and vibrant leader with moral vision and courage, the book documents Kennedy's physical illnesses which often debilitated him and the now well-known immorality which seemed to have characterized his life-style. During recent political campaigns, we have once again observed the question of character debated regarding major political candidates.

The question remains, "Is one qualified to lead without moral and spiritual character?"

Nehemiah has a clear answer to that question.

> 1 And there was a great outcry of the people and their wives against their Jewish brethren. 2 For there were those who said, "We, our sons, and our daughters are many; therefore let

us get grain for them, that we may eat and live." *3* There were also some who said, "We have mortgaged our lands and vineyards and houses, that we might buy grain because of the famine."   *4* There were also those who said, "We have borrowed money for the king's tax on our lands and vineyards.   *5* Yet now our flesh is as the flesh of our brethren, our children as their children; and indeed we are forcing our sons and our daughters to be slaves, and some of our daughters are brought into slavery already. It is not in our power to redeem them, for other men have our lands and vineyards."   *6* And I became very angry when I heard their outcry and these words.   *7* After serious thought, I rebuked the nobles and rulers, and said to them, "Each of you is exacting usury from his brother." So I called a great assembly against them.   *8* And I said to them, "According to our ability we have re-deemed our Jewish brethren who were sold to the nations. Now indeed, will you even sell your brethren? Or should they be sold to us?" Then they were silenced and found nothing to say.   *9* Then I said, "What you are doing is not good. Should you not walk in the fear of our God because of the reproach of the nations, our ene-mies?   *10* I also, with my brethren and my ser-vants, am lending them money and grain. Please, let us stop this usury!   *11* Restore now to them, even this day, their lands, their vine-yards, their olive groves, and their houses, also the hundredth part of the money and the grain, the new wine and the oil, that you have charged them."   *12* So they said, "We will re-store it, and will require nothing from them; we will do as you say." Then I called the priests, and required an oath from them that they would do according to this promise. *13* Then I shook out the fold of my garment and said, "So may God shake out each man from his house, and from his property, who does not perform this promise. Even thus may he be shaken out and emptied." And all the congregation said, "Amen!" and praised the Lord. Then the people did according to this promise (5:1-13).

This is a classic text on the question of character. What is the question of character I want to present and answer? It reveals the way we handle money often reveals inner character. Believe me, that's not the most popular subject in the world. How are you mastering your money? There is no surer barometer or measurement of character than how we handle our material possessions. We will either master our money and possessions or we will be mastered by them. We will either handle what God allows to enter our hands, and handle them well as faithful stewards, or we will mishandle them to our deep regret.

Here we see the *problem of mismanagement* of money, but we also see the principles of *mastering our money*. It is a question of character. There are over 2,000 verses in the Word of God that speak directly to this subject. Jesus Christ had more to say about material possessions and how we use them than He spoke of heaven and hell combined— because even in the management of a commodity so common and temporal as money, it is related to that which is eternal and in heaven. That is why Jesus taught, "Don't lay up treasures only on

things below, but on things above. Lay your treasures up in heaven" (see Matt. 6:19-20).

We are going to run into several people who were
mastered by their money. We meet them in these
verses. They were in financial bondage. As a result,
verse 1 tells us there was division among the children of Israel. They were moving right along building that wall, and then arose a crisis over
management of money. There was a problem that
could have forced tearing down the wall or failure
to complete it. The devil often causes division over
this subject and issue in families, in churches, and
in government. There was a shortage of human ne-
cessities and there were high prices (v. 2).

In verse 3, we meet these Israelites who were
mortgaged up to their ears. Is this beginning to
sound familiar to any of us? In verse 4, we note
there was the problem of debt. They were borrowing money, just to get by, even to pay their taxes.
With this word is a caution to all of us about exces-
sive borrowing and indebtedness. The Bible has
several very clear statements about overextending
ourselves and committing ourselves and borrowing. The Bible does not specifically, in my estimation, prohibit borrowing, but it certainly teaches we
ought to pay our debts. In Psalm 37:21: "The
wicked borrow and do not repay, but the righteous
show mercy and give."

The reason many people today are facing financial difficulties is because debt—easy credit—
makes it possible for us to fund our greed rather
than simply to fund our need. The Jews were up,
over, and under. Indebtedness. We need always to
be asking ourselves, "Am I using my money merely

to fund what I want, when I want it, right now, or
am I using the money God provides to meet the real
needs of my life and those of others?" If you borrow
money, the scriptural principle is: you must borrow
money only if you have the guarantee to pay it
back. Owe no man anything. That is, when the bill
comes due, pay it.

I heard about a revival out in the Oklahoma
country. The banker in that little town was not a
Christian, never darkened the door of a church, but
he mentioned to some of his friends at the coffee
shop, "You know, these Christians are really having
a revival down at the church."

"How do you know?" they inquired.

"Because all of the Christians are paying their
bills!" That's real revival!

Nehemiah's people were in severe bondage to
debt. As a result, (v. 5), we discover they were totally in financial slavery. They were mortgaging the
future of their children due to their financial condition. (Does that sound like our nation? The U.S. is
four trillion dollars in debt!) They said, "We are selling our children into slavery we are in such debt."
Many people today would see themselves there because they are in financial bondage. Bondage is not
God's will for His people. Jesus said, "You shall
know the truth, and the truth shall set you free"
(John 8:32). Freedom and liberty. Where the Spirit
of the Lord is, there is liberty. If you read Deuter-
onomy 28, the Bible promises blessing after blessing after blessing, not bondage to His people. God
has delivered His people out of bondage through
Jesus Christ and unto blessing. But the devil wants
to keep you in bondage. Sometimes he uses our fi-

nances to put us in financial bondage so we cannot be free to serve the Lord God.

Do you want to know whether or not you are in financial bondage?

Checklist for Financial Bondage

1. When you charge daily expenditures because of a lack of funds, you are in financial bondage.

2. When you must put off paying a bill until next month because you can't pay it this month, you are in financial bondage.

3. When you borrow to pay fixed expenses (i.e., your house or mortgage payment, light bill, taxes) you are in financial bondage.

4. When you become unaware of how much you owe, you are in financial bondage.

5. When you have creditors calling you and writing you about past-due bills, you are in financial bondage.

6. When you take from savings accounts to pay current bills, you are in financial bondage.

7. When you make new loans to pay off old loans, you are in financial bondage.

8. When you and your spouse argue about finances, you are in financial bondage.

Some marriages have to say not "Until *death* do us part" but "Until *debt* do us part!" When you find your family divided by arguments and frustrations over finances, that is bondage.

9. When you consider being dishonest, unscrupulous, or unethical about your finances, you are in financial bondage. If the thought, the suggestion, or the idea of being dishonest enters your

mind in order to meet the demands of pressures on your finances, that is bondage.

10. When you find it difficult to return God's tithe to God's house on God's day, you are in financial bondage. Many who love the Lord, who belong to Jesus Christ, find themselves in this kind of a struggle.

As a result, in the Book of Nehemiah, the saints of God were turning on one another. It was because of the pressure of finances. That is common. For example, if you begin talking about money in the church, people who are struggling with this issue, people who are under such pressure in this area, find the irritation rising up within them, and may even become angry because someone preached or taught about money in the church. That is the result of the bondage rather than the blessing of financial freedom.

It was the devil's strategy to divide the people over money and to stop the work of God. That is still his plan. How often he uses money in our lives to master us and control us in order to limit the work of Jesus Christ in our lives and in our churches. But it wasn't only those who were having a hard time that were in financial bondage, not just the poor and distraught, not just those who could not pay their bills, but there was another group which was also in fiscal chains. That was the group of nobles Nehemiah confronted, those who had money and were using it to manipulate the poor. They were exacting exorbitant, usurious interest rates from their own people who were borrowing barely enough to get by. Nehemiah was outraged. He sat down, collected himself, and said, "I became very angry" (v. 6). After verse 7, he didn't blow his stack. After serious thought, he presented the idea to the nobles, that they would correct this matter, which they did.

The point I am making is: these were men in financial bondage, not the bondage of need, but the bondage of greed. That is an onerous bondage because money is a wonderful servant, but it is also a terrible master. Here were men mastered by their money, by their greeds, by their covetousness. That is why Jesus warned, "Beware of covetousness: for a man's life consisteth not in the abundance of the things which he possesseth" (Luke 12:15, KJV).

Do you want to know whether you are letting your greed catch up to you and control you? Ask yourself these questions:

1. Do I think more of money than I think of God? How to make it, how to keep it, how to gain, how to get it.

2. Do I have goals and ambitions that do not square with the will of God? William Cook has a wonderful definition of success in his book, *Success, Motivation, and the Scriptures:* "Success is the continual adjustment of my life to God-given goals."[1]

3. Do I have a burning desire and love for money and to "get rich quick"? The Bible says, "The love of money is the root of all evil" (1 Tim. 6:10). The love of money, the love of things, the passion for position, and the pursuit for possessions. The desire to get rich quick.

While I am on this subject, let me touch on the lottery. The lottery is a "get-rich-quick" scheme for both the government and others who abuse it. When I was in Florida, the state voted in the lottery, unfortunately, and the promise was the state would have huge revenues for education. To this day Florida educators are asking, "Where is all of this money we were promised?" The lottery sadly preys upon the poor and the worst ambitions of people. No state with a lottery is any better off financially now than it was pre-lottery. I believe that any scheme to get rich quick is contrary to the Word of God. Proverbs 28:20 says, "A faithful man shall abound with blessings: but he that maketh haste to be rich shall not be innocent."

Do you compromise the Christian ethic and fail to honor your moral obligations? Is there any inkling of dishonesty in your life? If there is, that is bondage. No matter how much money we may have, some are poor in bondage, and some are rich in bondage, but it is still bondage. Mastered by money.

What was Nehemiah's solution? How do we master our money? There are three principles in verses 14-18 that show us how to master our money rather than to be mastered by it.

The first principle is:

First Things First

Look at verses 14-15:

Moreover, from the time that I was appointed to be their governor in the land of Judah, from the twentieth year until the thirty-second year of

King Artaxerxes, twelve years, neither I nor my
brothers ate the governor's provisions. But the
former governors who had been before me laid
burdens on the people, and took from them
bread and wine, besides forty shekels of silver;
yes, even their servants bore rule over the people,
but I did not do so, because of the fear of God.

Nehemiah had now become the governor of Judah, appointed by King Artaxerxes of the Persians,
but he refused to profit from his position. He was in
control and in charge, but he refused to take money
and provision for his service. He laid aside his personal rights to put God first. He wrote, "I feared the
Lord." He was living by the New Testament precept,
"Seek ye first the kingdom of God and His righteousness, and all these things shall be added unto
you" (Matt. 6:33). It was the matter of Lordship in
his life. The Lord was interested and involved in his
finances, so Nehemiah refused to lay up treasures
on earth at the expense of laying up treasures in
heaven. If money is our God, we will never be free.
Money is an idol that will devour its worshipers.
When we come to Christ, we must come with all we
have.

Sam Houston, the great Texan, won the battle of
San Jacinto and the liberation of Texas. Later on in
life, he came to Christ. A Baptist preacher, along
with the congregation, went down to a creek to
baptize Houston. There in profession of his faith in
Christ, that great Texan was baptized in the name
of the Father, the Son, and the Holy Spirit. When he
came up, he reached into his pocket, pulled out his
wallet, and announced to the preacher, "Well, Reverend, it looks like you baptized my pocketbook,

too!" Has your baptism included your pocketbook? It did for Sam Houston, whether intentionally or not. That is a priority. First things first.

Nehemiah had integrity. In verse 16, he stated, "I continued to work on the wall." He continued to work. By the way, the reason many people have no opportunities and have no money is because some people recognize an opportunity even if it comes dressed in work clothes. Nehemiah challenged the people to *work*. There were industry and integrity. Also in verse 16, he said, "We did not buy any land." What does that mean? Nehemiah couldn't have bought land cheap and taken advantage of others. He could have profited personally, but he was completely honest in his financial dealings. Why? First things first. God must be first in all we have and all we are.

The second principle:

More Blessed to Give Than to Receive

Look at verse 17: "Moreover there were at my table one hundred and fifty Jews and rulers, besides those who came to us from the nations around us." Now he began to entertain and host those around him. "Now that which was prepared for me daily was one ox and six choice sheep; also fowl were prepared for me, and once every ten days an abundance of all kinds of wine; yet in spite of this I did not demand the governor's provisions, because the bondage was heavy on this people" (v. 18).

He had learned the New Testament principle that "it is more blessed to give than to receive" (Acts 20:35). He was generous. He had one hundred and fifty guests for dinner for twelve straight years.

How would you like that, ladies? They ate fine fare. It wasn't beans out of a can. He fed over and over again. God kept giving him the supply. He didn't take money from the people. He didn't unduly tax the people. God kept providing because he kept giving. He became a conduit of blessing. He had learned the Scripture, "Give and it shall be given unto you, good measure, pressed down, shaken together and running over" (Luke 6:38). He was addicted to giving. That is a good addiction.

That joy we experience at Christmas when we are giving can be experienced day by day if we learn how to give. The Bible says, "God loves a cheerful giver" (2 Cor. 9:7)—literally, *hilarious* giver. I am waiting for the day when the offering plates pass and a fellow turns to his wife and shouts, "Come on, Honey, let's give!" and applause or laughter breaks across the congregation. We ought to get excited, hilarious, about the opportunity, not just to get a blessing, but to be a blessing.

You might comment, "Well, if I had more money, I'd give more." Look, it is now how much we make that determines what kind of givers we are. The emphasis in the Bible is never on what we have, but on what we give. Worth is determined not by our wealth, but by our worship of Jesus Christ. If you want to know what a man's worth, don't ask that man, "What do you make?" Instead, ask that man, "What do you give?" That is the real measurement. Unfortunately, recent statistics in churches across America show that the average church member gives only 2.5 percent of their income to the work of the Lord. The same article suggested that if every member of the church went on welfare, and our salaries were all reduced to welfare wages, and we all tithed our welfare check, that the receipts of the church would double!

I am convinced that people who love Jesus Christ want to give. There is the desire to give, but the problem that many of us have is that we are in such bondage financially that we don't know how. We don't have a plan or a program to get out of debt and get into the joy of giving. In other words, we have the desire to give, but we don't have the design or the program. I would challenge you as families, as couples, as individuals to sit down with one another, along with your checkbook and your finances, and determine together how you can fit into God's plan of economy for your life. You need to unfetter yourselves from the financial chains that bind you. You can be free and liberated as a servant of Jesus Christ.

The Bible teaches proportionate and programmed giving. That is why the apostle Paul taught that on the first day of the week as each person had planned and been prospered, he was to bring the offering to the Lord (1 Cor. 16:1-2). Giving shouldn't happen just spontaneously when we are moved by some emotional appeal. Giving should be planned and proportionate according to God's way and God's will as revealed in Scripture. When you discover that joy and when you join God's program and God's plan, you are going to discover that your money is no longer mastering you, but you are mastering your money. Better yet, God will be mastering your money. It all begins when we are willing to let God bless us.

When my wife Deb and I were at Hardin-

Simmons (we were married students our last two years there) we had a little house we rented. It was student housing, actually old army barracks, but it was a haven to us as a young couple. I was pastor of a part-time church and made $40 a week. Deb had a job as a secretary in the PE department of the school. We had a little budget and were making it work. Another house down the street was for rent. It was a cute, white house with a little porch—and bigger. We looked at that house and said, "Wouldn't it be great if we could figure out how we could get into that house?" We started writing out how we could afford it on our budget. I believe the house was $70 a month instead of $54. So, we had it all figured out—down to the penny—how we could afford that house. Deb's parents visited us, and I took her dad, a strong Christian, committed churchman, to show him that house. And I said, "Here's the budget. I think we have it worked out so we can do this. Do you think that's right." He kept on looking at it and didn't say anything.

I asked, "Well, don't you think we can do this? Don't you think we can afford this house?"

He came back, "Well, Jack, I think you can, but there's only one thing that is missing here on your budget. I just don't see it. I don't see your tithe on here!"

"That's right," I answered. We made a decision as a young couple that we could stay in the old house and pay God and do what was right. I am not trying to make us sound pious, because we struggle in this even as many of you have struggled and are struggling in it. But you have to make a determination of what is right. You must not live your life based on your creditors, but upon what God wants you to do.

Mary Crowley is one of the most influential citizens in the history of Dallas. A grand Christian woman, she came to Dallas broke as a single parent. Her son Don, faithful member of our church, and his brothers and sisters had practically nothing. She got a job, I believe, washing dishes. They had to live on that. They got on the bus every Sunday, paid the fare, and went downtown to First Baptist Church. She led her family to love and honor Jesus Christ. They tithed their income. She would always set aside 75 cents extra a month because there were times when it would rain, and they had to ride a taxi. If they would reach the end of the month, and it had not rained, and they saved the 75 cents, Don was always wanting the money for something extra. It drove him wild because his mother would insist that the money belonged to God, and she put it in the offering plate every time. It is no wonder that God was able ultimately to financially prosper Mary Crowley and bless her beyond measure.

That kind of faith and commitment—because the principle of "it is more blessed to give than to receive"—means that:

You Cannot Outgive God

Nehemiah depended upon God to supply his every need, and God did. You put God first in your life, in your finances, and I promise God will take care of you. You can't outgive God. That is how to master your money.

The highest expression of giving is the simplicity

of John 3:16. "For God so loved the world that He gave His only begotten Son." Paul exulted, "Thanks be unto God for His indescribable, unspeakable gift" (see 2 Cor. 9:15). Paul had a tremendous vocabulary. Yet, when it came to the gift of God, the salvation that he found in Jesus Christ, he said, "I can't even describe it. Just thank you, Lord, for Your indescribable gift." That gift was bought and purchased on the cross when Jesus died for you and me, and rose again that we might receive the free gift of eternal life.

If our greatest need had been information, God would have sent an educator. If our greatest need had been technology, God would have sent a scientist. If our greatest need had been money, God would have sent an economist. If our greatest need had been pleasure, God would have sent an entertainer. But because our greatest need was forgiveness, God sent a Savior, even Jesus Christ, that He might give eternal life to us. Rather than our becoming greedy getters, we become gracious givers.

Note

1. William Cook, *Success, Motivation, and the Scriptures* (Nashville: Broadman Press, 1974).

9

Compromise

Nehemiah 6:1-4

When Nehemiah heard that the walls were down, it, of course, staggered him. It brought him to his knees, and he prayed, "Oh, God, I don't know how. I don't even know why, but somehow let me be a part of the solution to this problem." Nehemiah volunteered himself and offered, "God, if you equip me and send me, I will go to Jerusalem, there to establish and rebuild the walls, and the city will once again reflect Your glory."

The walls stood for separation and protection; they were a testimony to the greatness and the glory of God. Broken, shattered walls did not speak well for the God of Israel. So, Nehemiah accepted God's call and was provided with resources to go. He gathered and challenged the people, and they responded, "We will rise up and build." The walls began to go up. Throughout the building of those walls there arose opposition of all kinds, the subtle and not so subtle attacks launched to destroy the work of God. There were ridicule, force, slander, intimidation, manipulation, lies, treachery, and fraud. In chapter 6, one of the most insidious tactics of the devil came in an attempt to destroy the man of God and the work of God. What was that tactic? Compromise. In Nehemiah 6:1-4, we discover what happened.

> 1 Now it happened when Sanballat, Tobiah, Geshem the Arab, and the rest of our enemies heard that I had rebuilt the wall, and there were no breaks in it (though at that time I had not hung the doors in the gates), 2 that Sanballat and Geshem sent to me, saying, "Come, let us meet together in one of the villages in the plain of Ono." But they thought to do me harm. 3 So I sent messengers to them, saying, "I am doing a great work, so that I cannot come down. Why should the work cease while I leave it and go down to you?" 4 But they sent me this message four times, and I answered them in the same manner.

Satan hates God's success. When the people of God say, "Let us arise and build," the enemy will say, "Let us arise and blast." So these devices of the enemy, one power play after another, were used against Nehemiah and the children of Israel. Yet, the wall was completed, except that the doors of the gates were not yet hung. There was still an entry point into the city. Paul wrote: "Neither give place to the devil" (Eph. 4:27). Don't give the devil a foothold. Don't give the devil a place to get in, an entrance. So Nehemiah was aware the job was not finished, and yet the enemy came trying to enter that one place of vulnerability.

A marathon is twenty-six miles, 385 yards.

Those who run marathons declare that the last 300-plus yards is the most difficult challenge of the entire race—finishing the course. So it was with Nehemiah. All could have been lost and the battle lost had he given up at that point. Therefore, the final attack came, and Nehemiah and the people needed to respond. The tactic was that of compromise. "Come down. Let's get together." It was repeated four times. It is given to us in verse 7 and again in verse 10. "Let us get together. Let us negotiate." The place was to be the plains of Ono. Geographically, that is halfway between the city of Jerusalem and Samaria. "Let us meet halfway," the enemy offered, "and let's talk about it. Nehemiah, why are you such a separatist? Why are you so hard-nosed? Let us negotiate and moderate this situation. Let's compromise."

There are times when the right kind of compromise can be positive. Compromise is necessary in human relations of all sorts. You know it is certainly true in your marriage. You'd better learn how to compromise. In business and in life, learning how to negotiate and mediate is vitally important, when it does not affect spiritual, biblical, moral, or ethical issues. Compromise is positive until it begins to affect and impact our moral and spiritual convictions. We dare not live by the adage, "Peace at any price."

When it comes to truth and to our testimony, there is no place to negotiate or compromise. Be careful about sleeping with the enemy and negotiating with the enemy.

I heard about a hunter who was chasing a bear, trying to shoot him for a fur coat for winter wear.

The bear, finally out of breath, stopped and asked, "Wait a minute, let's talk about this. You want a fur coat, and all I want is a meal. Let's sit down and talk about it." So, the hunter thought that was reasonable. He sat down and talked about it with the bear. Sure enough the bear had a meal, and the hunter wore a fur coat—only not quite as he had anticipated.

Compromise can be deadly. I am convinced that it has ruined more churches, diluted more messages, neutralized more preachers, and weakened more Christians than any other factor. Compromise can be devastating and could have led to the destruction of the wall and the project and all that Nehemiah was trying to do. "Come down, let's get together. Let's talk about this thing." Now when you are tempted to compromise, think of three considerations Nehemiah remembered. To overcome the temptation to compromise we must remember:

The Purity of Our Faith

On what basis could Nehemiah get together with those enemies? These were the same devil's advocates who lied about him, sought to destroy him, threatened him, taunted him, and would have assassinated him. He had absolutely nothing in common with those men. So, Nehemiah practiced godly, biblical separation which is the clear teaching of the Word of God. It is taught in the Old Testament by example and precept. For example, Amos, "Can two walk together except they be agreed?" (Amos 3:3). It is taught plainly in the New Testament. For example, look at 2 Corinthians 6:14-16:

Do not be unequally yoked together with unbelievers. For what fellowship has righteousness with lawlessness? And what communion has light with darkness? And what accord has Christ with Belial? Or what part has a believer with an unbeliever? And what agreement has the temple of God with idols? For you are the temple of the living God.

See 2 Corinthians 7:1: "Therefore, having these promises, beloved, let us cleanse ourselves from all filthiness of the flesh and spirit, perfecting holiness in the fear of God."

This is an unmistakable biblical principle of godly, separated living, a life-style that is set apart. We have no community, commonality, and continuity with people who do not receive Jesus Christ, who deny Jesus Christ as God. We certainly cannot work together with them. Yes, we can work together with those who disagree on minor issues, nonessentials of the faith, those matters of interpretation that aren't tests of fellowship. Yet, there are certain non-negotiables of the Christian faith—the Deity of Jesus Christ; the authority and infallability of the Word of God; the blood atonement, that is, the substitutionary death by His blood for our sins on the cross; His bodily resurrection; salvation by grace through faith; and the doctrine of the Trinity: the Father, the Son, and the Holy Spirit. We are to earnestly contend for the faith which was once for all delivered for the saints.

We must not compromise our convictions, to bend our beliefs to suit the enemy. We must realize we have no point of reference or basis for agreement. Now, humanly speaking we can and should get together with unbelievers for community projects, for crisis responses in the community. There are many points of contact we can share humanly in the workplace, but when it comes to our faith, morality, our ethics—what is right and what is wrong, what is true and what is not true—there is no room for compromise.

When we are tempted to compromise, we should think of:

The Responsibility of Our Work

Back in Nehemiah 6, Nehemiah realized the importance and value of his own work. He said in verse 3, "So I sent messengers to them, saying, 'I am doing a great work, so that I cannot come down. Why should the work cease while I leave it and go down to you?'" He repeats that in verses 10 and 11. Nehemiah was not suggesting that it was a great work because he was doing it, but because God was doing it. This was the work of God. If you are serving Jesus Christ, your work is a great work. The hymn goes, "Every work for Jesus will be blest." If you abandon the work and quit what God has called you to do, you are stepping down. Maybe you are a Sunday School teacher and say, "Well, I have only five or six in my class." It is a great work; it is God's work. Perhaps you are a homemaker or mother, and you alibi, "I'm just a homemaker." Dear lady, it is a great work to be a mother to your children and a homemaker. Perhaps you are a witness to church visitors, and you are knocking on those doors in bad weather, and you are wondering if it is really worth it and if you should keep going. Friend, it is a great work.

Nehemiah refused to become sidetracked. He

refused to detour onto avenues of his own choosing or worse, letting others choose paths for him. He made it terse, "I cannot come down. Why should I leave the work and come down to you?" In the church of Jesus Christ today, we must maintain consistency with our mission. At our church, I pray we have a reputation in this community and this state as keeping the main emphasis out front—bringing people to Jesus Christ, baptizing them, maturing and equipping them in Christian living. As a pastor and people, we refuse to become involved in agendas that carry us off into side-streets and sideroads and call us away from the great work God has called us to do. We will "stay by the stuff," bringing people to Jesus Christ.

Nehemiah said, "Oh, no" to Ono. "I'm not going down to Ono." That should be the response of every Christian. If it is true for the church it is true personally. Our choices in life as Christians are not so much between what is right or wrong, good or bad, but what is good, better, or best. There are thousands of good things you and I could be doing. Under God you must determine what He wants you to do, and center in on what He wants, not forty things you dabble at. Consider that when you are tempted to compromise.

Finally, consider:

The Integrity of Our Witness

Folks were watching Nehemiah. The project was dependent upon his faithful execution of leadership. If he had gone down, it could have sabotaged the whole project. A bad decision by a good man is far worse than a bad decision by a bad man. Nehemiah, God's man, recognized his example. Their enemies came at him again and again and again. I am sort of reminded of the Road Runner cartoons. Do you remember Wiley Coyote? He always was devising fiendish traps for the Road Runner. He kept coming and coming and coming after him, but the Road Runner always had the last "beep, beep." Nehemiah had the last "beep, beep." He said it four times, "I will not come down. I will not give in. I will not compromise. I will not capitulate."

Here is the point. Leadership and Christian living today demand decisive action. Make your decision about what you believe, about what is right, about what is truth, and stay by it. So many people live by opinions. We have all of these opinion polls today. Everyone seems to have an opinion. Very few have convictions. Do you know the difference between an opinion and a conviction? An opinion is something we "hold." A conviction is something that "holds" us. It grips your heart and will not let you go. Mary Crowley used to say that one person with a belief is greater than ninety-nine with a casual interest—one person with a belief, not just opinions, not just preferences that change with the wind.

Christians in this generation must take decisive action, know what they believe, and why they believe what they believe biblically, morally, ethically. I have a saying I use with my children. I share it in counseling situations time and time again. *It is always right to do right. It is never wrong to do right. It is never right to do wrong.* What is right is right, and under God, his people, like Nehemiah, must take their stand and stick to their position. If our position is of God and grace, let us stay with it.

That is why Nehemiah was a leader. He had courage. He had backbone. Too many people have a yellow streak where their backbone ought to be.

To show you, case and point, the kind of courage he had, remember chapter 5. Loansharking was going on, and the wealthy people were robbing and extorting the poor people in Israel. His speaking out against that usury could have absolutely destroyed the project, so Nehemiah was on the horns of the dilemma. Why? Because Nehemiah needed the support of that wealthy crowd. He needed those nobles to be with him through their financial and prayer support. He needed those wealthy aristocrats who were fleecing the poor people. So, what was Nehemiah to do? Sweep it under the rug, ignore it, turn his head, look the other way? Not Nehemiah.

After he had considered it, he confronted face to face and challenged those who were robbing the poor. He could have lost it all. He did not lose his integrity. As a result of his willingness to stand for and do what was right, the nobles confessed, "Nehemiah, you're right. We repent. We'll change this." How many people have dreams, creative thoughts, and commitments that are never acted out just because their convictions are often for sale? Whittier wrote: "The saddest words of tongue or pen are these, It might have been." Think of what could happen if we only followed through on our dreams, resolutions, and commitments. If so, the world would be full of heroes. So often, we sell out too quickly and too cheaply and settle for less than the best.

Daniel Webster was considered one of the most

brilliant and eloquent statesmen of the nineteenth century. He was an American political idol, so much so that in 1831, Ralph Waldo Emerson wrote concerning him, "Let Webster's lofty face ever on thousands shine a beacon set that freedom's race might gather amens from the radiant sign." What a man was Daniel Webster! Webster had political aspirations to become the President of the United States. He sought the nomination of his party to become the President. In order to gain the nomination, he accommodated his views on slavery. Previously, he had opposed slavery, but in order to garner votes, he compromised his values. As a result, he never was elected President, and his brightly shining political star was extinguished. Twenty-three years after Emerson had written those original words, Emerson sadly penned these words concerning his friend Webster. "Why did all manly gifts in Webster fail? He wrote on nature's grandest brow 'for sale.'"

How many Christians have written "for sale" on their brows and values, selling out and negotiating their testimony for nothing! In these latter days before Christ returns, you will be tempted to compromise like never before, to rethink what you believe about this Bible, to reevaluate your faith, your values, your commitments, your virtues, and your morality. The devil will tempt you to moderate and capitulate to him.

But before you do that, stop and think. Consider The purity of your Faith, the responsibility of your work, and the integrity of your witness. Let us assert with Martin Luther when he stood before a papal tribunal, "Here I stand. I can do no other."

10

The Acid Test

Nehemiah 6

Nehemiah's model of ministry is certainly one of the greatest examples of leadership in all of human history. As the walls were being rebuilt, Nehemiah exhibited characteristics of courage and conviction. In spite of numerous obstacles and the opposition's attempts to discredit God's man and distort and destroy God's work, this man and his people stood tall and completed the job in fifty-two days. Just before the job was completed, one final assault was launched. It was the "acid test," the final trial of Nehemiah's leadership and ministry. The threat was that of slander and of sin.

The devil is a liar and a murderer. His intention is always to defeat what God desires to do in and through our lives. So, one more time the enemy attacked God's man.

Attack from the Accuser

5 Then Sanballat sent his servant to me as before, the fifth time, with an open letter in his

hand.   *6* In it was written: It is reported among
the nations, and Geshem says, that you and the
Jews plan to rebel; therefore, according to these
rumors, you are rebuilding the wall, that you
may be their king.   *7* And you have also appointed prophets to proclaim concerning you at
Jerusalem, saying, "There is a king in Judah!"
Now these matters will be reported to the king.
So come, therefore, and let us take counsel together.   *8* Then I sent to him, saying, "No such
things as you say are being done, but you invent
them in your own heart."   *9* For they all were
trying to make us afraid, saying, "Their hands
will be weakened in the work, and it will not be
done." Now therefore, O God, strengthen my
hands.   *10* Afterward I came to the house of
Shemaiah the son of Delaiah, the son of Meheta-
beel, who was a secret informer; and he said,
"Let us meet together in the house of God,
within the temple, and let us close the doors
of the temple, for they are coming to kill
you; indeed, at night they will come to kill
you."   *11* And I said, "Should such a man as I
flee? And who is there such as I who would go
into the temple to save his life? I will not go
in!"   *12* Then I perceived that God had not sent
him at all, but that he pronounced this prophecy
against me because Tobiah and Sanballat had
hired him.   *13* For this reason he was hired,
that I should be afraid and act that way and sin,
so that they might have occasion for an evil report, that they might reproach me.   *14* My God,
remember Tobiah and Sanballat, according to
these their works, and the prophetess Noadiah
and the rest of the prophets who would have
made me afraid.   *15* So the wall was finished on
the twenty-fifth day of the month of Elul, in fifty-

two days. *16* And it happened, when all our enemies heard of it, and all the nations around us saw these things, that they were very disheartened in their own eyes; for they perceived that this work was done by our God (vv. 5-16).

Threats of slander, violence, and even of murder were aimed at Nehemiah and his people. We should consider the source of the enemies that perpetrated one final assault and approach to God's man and God's work. They were simply representatives of a greater enemy who still attacks today. The devil is a liar and a murderer (see John 8:44). He was "a liar from the beginning and a murderer"— think of anything bad, and the devil is its daddy—a liar from the beginning when he slithered into the Garden of Eden with the subtlety of a snake and tempted Adam and Eve. Thus, sin entered the world. He is murderous, treacherous, and violent like "a roaring lion seeking those whom he may devour" (1 Pet. 5:8). He is the devourer, the adversary, the accuser; his method is to lie and his motive is murder. Satan's treacherous and violent lies are everywhere today.

The "safe-sex" lie has spread like lightning across society, and the result is Satan's method, and murder is his aim. "The wages of sin is death" (Rom. 6:23a). We must be on guard when the liar, accuser, and slanderer moves against us. Like Nehemiah, respond positively. How did Nehemiah respond, first of all, to that which we call slander?

Counterattack from the Christian

Verses 5-9 deal with this slander. Nehemiah stood as an example of believers, Christians, through the centuries. This affront was on the heels of the temptation when Nehemiah was called to come down and compromise on the planes of Ono. When he refused to compromise, it enraged his enemies. When he stood strong, an assault followed in the form of personal attack. Those enemies could not break Nehemiah's will so they sought to break his spirit with personal slams against him. It is childish when you think about it, but so often we recognize it today when folks who cannot handle issues respond by attacking others.

These charges levied against Nehemiah were full-blown, blatant lies. They were spreading this lie: "The report has come that you want to be the king. The rebuilding of this wall is for your own personal advancement. Nehemiah, you are a egomaniac. You want to be a dictator, an autocrat. You are in this for yourself." Just the opposite was true concerning Nehemiah. He was a sacrificial servant who left his featherbed in Persia and took a sleeping blanket, becoming a contractor after he was a cupbearer, leading in the rebuilding of the walls at personal risk.

With self-denial, he was feeding people at his own table. He refused to collect taxes for his own personal aggrandizement, yet this slanderous and treacherous lie was spread abroad. When a leader does anything for God, when someone stands for truth and righteousness, he is often accused of being bigoted, dictatorial, or close-minded. As always, a slanderous tongue is a powerful weapon in the hand of the enemy. The very word used in the Bible for slander is closely related to the word often translated for the devil, the slanderer. Gossip, rumoring, and backbiting are a national pastime. The *National Inquirer* has the largest circulation of any paper in the country. Why? Because people enjoy the gossip. Unfortunately, many Christians are chief proponents. They think they have conquered all the big sins. "I don't commit adultery. I don't murder anybody. I don't rob banks. It's just a little thing. I just like a juicy, little bit of gossip, or I just like to spread a tale every now and then." God declares, "I hate the perverted mouth" (Prov. 8:13c).

George Harrison, the former Beatle, wrote a song entitled, "The Devil's Radio." That was an appropriate title, for the devil does have his own broadcasting system. The late Marvin Gaye is best known for his hit "I Heard It Through the Grapevine." Let me strongly urge in the church of Jesus Christ that we prune that vine, the grapevine of gossip. Be extra careful. In Matthew 12:36, Jesus warned that at the judgment we will give an account of every careless word we have spoken.

God notes our words when our tongues are slanderous. Neither should we use our ears as garbage cans for somebody else's gossip or rumoring. When someone is slandered in your presence, what do you do? When you hear an evil report on one of God's leaders or a friend in the family of God, what is your response? May I urge you to believe the best about that person. That is how love responds. "Love hopes all things, believes all things, endures all things" (see 1 Cor. 13).

I have discovered a most practical way to stop the onslaught of the rumor mill. The next time someone passes along questionable information, why not ask, "May I quote you on that?" Or the next time you hear the "they-said" rumor, simply ask, "Who is they?" If people won't sign their name to it or stand up for something that is true, it is not worth hearing. Anonymous letters are examples of extreme cowardice. If someone sends a letter of criticism and refuses to sign it, it shouldn't even be read. Now if a person has the courage to confront us with facts and with criticism, then all of us need to respond in humility and ask God for the truth that may be in any criticism. Generally, in any criticism we receive, there may be a kernel of truth. We ought to unhusk it, find out what it is, and then ask God to help us grow. Nehemiah responded to lies. Let me give you an acrostic for when you are tempted to gossip, rumor, slander, or hear trash:

THINK

T: Is it TRUE?
H: Is it HELPFUL?
I: Is it IMPORTANT?
N: Is it NECESSARY?
K: Is it KIND?

Nehemiah, in verse 8, categorically denied the charges. He had a transparently clear conscience. His life was an open book. He simply asserted, "None of these things are true." He didn't make a case of himself. He didn't try to defend himself. He had the philosophy and platitude of Billy Graham. Years ago, when Mr. Graham was receiving personal attacks, he said, "No attack, no defense." When you are walking with and serving God, and your conscience is clear, you can plainly respond to all personal attacks. Nehemiah responded because

he knew that the devil wanted to weaken his hands
(v. 6). When unfair and untrue criticism ensues, it
can sap us of strength. When it hits you, remember
the words of Jesus, "Blessed are you when men
shall revile and persecute you and say all manner
of evil against you falsely for my sake. For so did
they persecute the prophets before you and great is
your reward in heaven" (see Matt. 5:11-12). When
the unfair and unjust criticisms sting, we realize if
we are doing it for Jesus' sake, it is a privilege to
suffer for Him, and great will be our reward. Therefore, we stay at the work. I love Nehemiah because
he was such a human being. He prayed, "Now,
therefore, God strengthen my hands."

Combating Sin

One final assault was the threat of sin. Verses 10-
14 deal with a conspiracy concocted to lure Nehemiah into the temple. A false prophet was hired to
visit Nehemiah and say, "Because these folks are
trying to kill you, you need to run into the temple
and hide." Nehemiah, full of faith and courage, responded in verse 11. "And I said, 'Should such a
man as I flee? And who is there such as I who
would go into the temple to save his life? I will not
go in!'" Nehemiah was solicited to commit sin. He
was a layman—not a priest—but a contractor and a
cupbearer. If Nehemiah had run fearfully for his life
into the temple and hidden in the sanctuary of
God, he would have broken God's commandment.
He was not a priest and had no business there. If he
had gone into the temple, then they really would
have had the goods on him. Verse 12: "Then I perceived that God had not sent him at all."

Nehemiah was a man of discrimination, discern-
ment, and perception. He realized that the man
who showed up with a so-called message from God
was not delivering a message from God at all. The
scripture advises us "to test (try) the spirits to see if
they are of God" (1 John 4:1). Many of God's people
today are gullible. They are susceptible and vulnerable to the lies of the enemy and his false prophets.
That is why it is so vital, Christian, that you be im-
mersed in the Word of the living God, that you
know the Book, that you love God's truth and study
it. Through the truth of God the Spirit of God is
able to set off the alarm when the lie comes, and
when the thief arises to steal the truth from your
life. Every Christian ought to be wired spiritually
with an alarm system that will protect him against
all who would lie and harm him with untruth.
Not everyone who speaks about God is of God.
Nehemiah perceived that. There are many false
prophets, philosophies, and doctrines even in the
church. I heard several years ago about a Hallow-
een Party at a church in North Carolina where the
minister of the church decided to dress up in a devil's suit. Can you imagine that? But guess what is
worse than that. It is a devil dressed up in a minister's suit!

The Bible declares that the devil even disguises
himself "as an angel of light" (see 2 Cor. 11:14).
Christians, beware and be warned. Lies and seduc-
tions, of course, are not from God. One of the proofs
that this was not from God was because it tried to
put fear in Nehemiah's heart. They suggested, "If
you're afraid you can run and hide in the temple."
He was positive that spirit didn't come from God,

1. *Concerning their faithfulness to the Word of God.* That is the essence of verse 29. They pledged, "We will live under the authority of God and His Word for our lives. We will live by the Book; we will not only hear the Word of God, we will do the Word of God. We will honor and heed the Word." "Trust and obey, for there's no other way; To be happy in Jesus, but to trust and obey." Therefore, they made a physical dedication to themselves and emphasized, "We will be a people of the Book." That is our covenant: to be a people of the Book.

2. *Concerning their families.* Verse 30 stresses, "We will not give our daughters as wives to the people of the land, nor take their daughters for our sons." They were making a specific covenant. They were making those promises and that pledge, citing this oath of obedience, public proclamation, and spiritual separation. They would consecrate themselves and their families. They were not going to let the world have their children. You as Christian moms, dads, grandparents, and guardians need to make the same commitment today. There is a fight for the family, and forces that oppose all we stand for as the church of Jesus Christ are seeking the minds, the hearts, and the wills of your children. It is time we believers joined in the battle and asserted, "We will not lose our children to the devil's crowd. We will dedicate ourselves, our marriages, our homes, our families to the living God. We will not allow our children to go the way of the world. We will fight and struggle for them." That was a commitment the Jews made.

3. *Concerning their finances.* Verse 31: "if the peoples of the land bring wares or any grain to sell on the Sabbath day . . ." Remember, they were be-

coming specific. They were going to demonstrate
that God had changed their lives. ". . . We would not
buy it from them on the Sabbath or a holy day."
They would make sure their money was going to be
rightfully gained. They were going to dedicate the
Sabbath Day to worship and later the Lord's Day.
No matter how good the deal was when the pagans
came in from another country, they would not do
business on the Lord's Day.

We should make a commitment to serve our God
on that day. We are not to gain our money dis-
honestly. That is an ironclad principle. They also
agreed that money was to be given generously.

They said, ". . . or on a holy day; and that we
would forego the seventh year's produce and the ex-
action of every debt. Also, we made ordinances for
ourselves, to exact from ourselves yearly one-third
of a shekel for the service of the house of our God."
The chapter goes on to describe the financial commitment they made. Verse 37: "to bring the
firstfruits of our dough, our offerings, the fruit from
all kinds of trees, the new wine and oil, to the
priests, the storerooms of the house of our God;
and to bring the tithes of our land to the Levites, for
the Levites should receive the tithes in all our farm-
ing communities." Verse 38: "Shall bring up a
tenth of the tithes to the house of our God, to the
rooms of the storehouse." What is this about?
Their commitment, dedication, and consecration
meant that it touched their pursestrings. They realized that the work and witness of God to the earth
meant financial commitment. They realized it took
money to carry on God's work, and so did Jesus
Christ. Our Lord said more about our pocketbooks

and our relationship to stewardship and financial dealings than any other person in all of the Bible.

He spoke words like, "Where your treasure is, there will your heart be also" (Matt. 6:21). The Jews of Nehemiah's day pledged, "We will generously give tithes and offerings unto the Lord." Why? Why should we? Because of what God means to us and what His work means to us. Because of all of this, we make a commitment and dedication concerning our finances. We bring our resources to make sure that God's house is not neglected. You ask, "Is that for the New Testament believer? Are we supposed to tithe? We don't have a temple?" Dear friend, the principle is the same. In view of the tender mercies of God in Christ, how can we do any less for His service? So, they made a dedication. So must we.

A man was complaining to a deacon in his church, "The church just costs too much."

And the deacon said, "Let me tell you a true story. A number of years ago a little boy was born into our home, a beautiful baby. Immediately, that child began to cost. There were diaper bills, food bills, milk bills, and all the costs that come with a baby.

"As the child grew, there was elementary school and all of those fees—soccer fees, football fees, you name it. All of the cost and all of the fees—and this kid began to eat us out of house and home. The boy decided he needed a car. We got him a car and put gasoline in it. It was costing us a fortune. We didn't have the money, but we sacrificed and did it because we loved that boy.

"Then the boy decided he wanted to go to college,

and we were poor for years sending him to college.
It cost us. Then in his senior year of college he was
killed in an automobile crash. Since that day our
boy hasn't cost us a dime! How I wish we had him
back so we could spend something on him!"

Anything that is alive costs us, and that which is
precious and valuable requires commitment. If the
church is to be alive, it is to be a vital influence in a
world without Jesus Christ. We need exactly the
sentiments of the children of Israel in the last
phrase of verse 39, "We will not neglect the house
of our God." We will pray, work, attend, and give as
we covenant together our faith, our families, and
our finances to the cause of Jesus Christ.